THE COMPOUNDER'S ELEMENT

A Patient Path to Prosperity

THE COMPOUNDER'S ELEMENT

A Patient Path to Prosperity

LAURENCE ENDERSEN

ISBN: 978-0-9930867-2-4
Published by Laurence Endersen
First Published 2024

Illustration and Production Design by Philip Barrett
www.blackshapes.com

In memory of Maureen Kennedy (1938– 2024).

Maureen had no interest in compounding capital, but she compounded love for over eight decades.

Contents

Acknowledgements

Thank you to fellow aspiring compounders for your thoughtful improvements and most of all your friendship. It's a privilege to accompany you on the patient path: Jeff Annello, Alan Burke, Paul Buser, Paul Ciampa, Aidan Corcoran, Sarah Endersen, Jonathan Escott, John Forde, David Henry, Patrick McNulty, John O'Brien, Niall O'Sullivan, Kris Powell, Paul Reidy and Karthik Tiruvarur.

I'd also like to thank friends who originally helped with one or more of the individual investment reflections that eventually found their way into this book: Barry Brennan, Paul Higgins, Stefan Jibodh, Kevin McMahon, Blas Moros, Rory O'Farrell, William Oliver, and Shane Parrish.

About the Author

Laurence Endersen originally studied law as a pathway to practicing taxation while also training as a chartered accountant. A move to Sydney, Australia in 1994 facilitated a career change to corporate advisory and project finance, before returning to Ireland in 1998 where he subsequently held a series of investment management roles across venture capital, structured securities, leveraged loans and listed equities. Laurence founded a private investment firm in 2015.

He currently lives with his family in Dublin.

Laurence has published two other books.

Pebbles of Perception: How a Few Good Choices Make all the Difference

What Owen Didn't Know: A Philosophical Fable

Introduction

People don't need extraordinary insight or intelligence. What they need most is the character to adopt simple rules and stick to them.

– Ben Graham

I'm fascinated by investment markets and have been for over thirty years. I love the nature of the work. One might observe that I am *in my element*. In ancient philosophy, people were thought to have a dominant element that defined their personality. Being in one's element meant being in an environment that aligned with one's inherent nature. The origins of elemental resonance can be traced back to the concept of the four classical elements: earth, water, air, and fire. This theory, which was prominent in ancient Greece, proposed that these elements were the fundamental building blocks of nature, and that each person had a particular affinity for, or balance of, these elements that constituted their physical and temperamental makeup. *The Compounder's Element* is about the patient pursuit of prosperity. It's a journey where the pursuit matters more than the prosperity, because when we are *in our element* the joy is in the journey.

It's said that one of the best ways to learn is to write. I've brought my own terminology and framing to what I've learned from others and from direct experience. Using one's own phrases helps solidify concepts and if the narrative is memorable those ideas may be useful more widely. Overarchingly, I've tried to capture the essence of things and in that spirit most of the chapters are short. A few are longer to avoid oversimplification of more nuanced topics. Some of the chapters overlap as common messages permeate multiple topics. We will investigate numerous investment themes, most of which an investor will encounter over their lifetime. My biggest realisation is that we overestimate what can be reliably achieved over the short-term, and underestimate what can be reliably achieved over the long term. That is not a novel concept, but due to the nature of compounding, it is particularly true of investing.

Who is this Book For?

This book is written for anyone interested in public markets investing, either on their own account or on behalf of others. It may also appeal to executives of public companies if they wish to better understand how they are viewed by stock market investors. For seasoned investors, the unconventional framing of multiple topics may allow readers see familiar concepts in new ways, sparking serendipitous avenues for deeper exploration.

Active stock picking is not for everyone. In fact, it's not a good idea for most people. An investment approach should resonate with one's skills, interests, and temperament. The investment journey is long, with frequent periods of poor performance, that we need to be able to navigate with equanimity. Our choice of game is crucial. Picking one for which we are neither emotionally suited nor practically competent makes no sense. In contrast to the increasingly quaint world of active stock picking, index fund investing or entrusting savings with independent fund managers have more universal appeal.* The beauty of the investment industry is that there are multiple paths to prosperity, but only when we match the path to our personality. We need to know who we are. What's unseen to us, the markets will eagerly enlighten.

The Patient Path

Building wealth slowly and assuredly, through a patient path to prosperity, is a path that's open to everyone. There are just a few key elements:

1. Plan for a long journey.
2. Enjoy the journey as its own reward.
3. Minimise the costs of mistakes along the way.

* While this book is about active stock picking, the Appendix has some pointers for choosing an investment manager. To understand investment asset classes beyond public securities, I recommend David Swensen's *Pioneering Portfolio Management*.

First and foremost, planning for a long journey speaks to the fundamental power of patience. The very deliberate act of choosing the patient path is what allows the conjoined twins of time and compounding to work their magic. Time is paradoxical.* One paradox of time is that it is both a leveller and a lever. We want to leverage time without being levelled by it. How do we position ourselves and our investments to align with time? We align best with time by being patient and slowing down, rather than trying to sprint our way through it on a thoughtless treadmill.

Secondly, to leverage time, we need to operate in harmony with it, respect it, understand it, cooperate with it, befriend it, and in so doing to enjoy the journey *as its own reward.* Time spent thinking, asking questions, patiently probing, and trying to understand how to operate in harmony with how the world really works, helps avoid bad decisions, the worst time sink of all.

Who accompanies us is just as important as where we are headed. A path taken in good company becomes a joyful one. I'd choose good company towards an average destination, over average company towards a good one. Thankfully, we don't have to choose, the patient path, by its very nature, attracts good company. No road is long with good company.

Avoiding bad decisions gets to the third key element; minimise the costs of mistakes along the way. Those costs are not just directly monetary. They turn up in time wasted, stress, reputational damage, and most of all the opportunity cost of falling off the patient productive path. Mistakes come from not

* Time is the great healer, and, in the end, we are all dead.

knowing what we are doing. Our job as investors, and in life, is to keep the consequences of our mistakes small. Let blunders be our tutors, not our tormentors, errors that illuminate, not eviscerate. Taking the careful, enjoyable and patient path is not for everyone, but those who do, will, absent bad luck,* almost assuredly become prosperous. If safe and steady long-term investing resonates, *you* will be *in your element.*

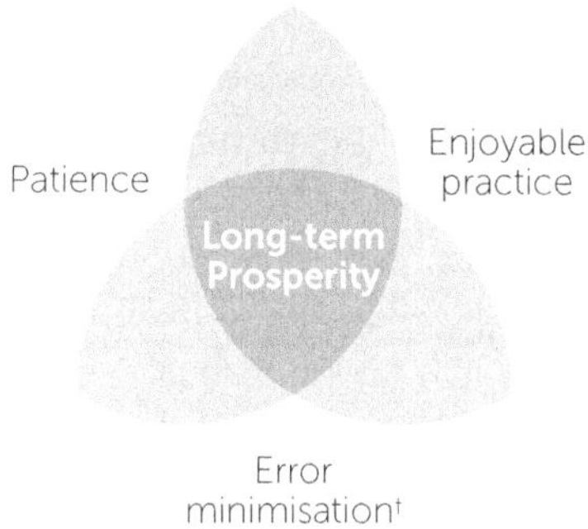

We are winning by not losing, a proven strategy more widely in areas like tennis, chess, health & safety, and military strategy. If you have played or watched non-elite tennis you will have noticed that the winner generally is the one who allows their opponent to 'lose first' (through their unforced errors).

* Unfortunately, nothing in life is assured. Every day that we get to live is tauntingly threatened by random events. Again, this is why we need to enjoy the journey as its own reward. That we even get to live at all is amazing. We forget this (echoing David Foster Wallace's fish; 'what the hell is water?')

† I really mean error consequence minimisation, or large error minimisation. Avoiding errors is unrealistic and undesirable. We must take some risks and survivable errors are a valuable source of information from which we can learn and adapt.

Beyond an examination of the fun in choosing, and staying on, the patient path, this book also dedicates some time to the identification of great businesses. If we are lucky enough to find one or two at a reasonable price, it can be financially transformational. Consider this a potential bonus. It's not necessary. Avoiding large mistakes, and staying on the path for long enough, will inevitably lead to prosperity. We don't need to find huge winners. But given the difference they could make, it would be remiss not to recognise one when we encounter it, so we can act decisively when the opportunity arises.

Structure

This book has four parts.

Part I takes first things first and looks at the choice to take the slow and steady path, and why that choice makes sense.

In **Part II** we explore the terrain by getting into the essence of core investment pillars like structurally advantaged business models, cash and optionality. The objective of Part II is to help us recognise a good thing when we see it.

Part III features the cliffs and the car crashes that can take us out, or slow us down. We meet the *miserable math of mistakes.*

Part IV concludes with some direct lessons from the road. These are interesting and practical topics that I've been reflecting on as a practitioner of the craft.

Let's dive in.

PART I
CHOOSING THE PATIENT PATH

The power of compounding is exponential and the only way to truly benefit from this exponential power is to survive for a long time. That's an iron law of mathematics. Like nature does, we should solve for survival, and if we want to solve for survival, we need to be patient. Survival doesn't believe in shortcuts. Nature doesn't borrow. As humans, we understand that good things take time, like a maturing Irish whiskey. But we are frequently blind to the exponential impact of compounding in the later years as our brains experience life linearly.

To frame the value of patience let's take the example of buying a house. Assume the house costs $100,000 and that you can borrow $70,000, so you must contribute $30,000. You buy the home, get to live in it and life goes on. Say that house prices in your area are increasing in value at a modest rate of 3% per annum. At some point, you decide to sell. When the time comes to sell, you intuitively know that you are going to have more than enough to pay back the bank and that you will have made a profit on your original $30,000 investment, but how much? And how does time come into the equation?

Let's look:

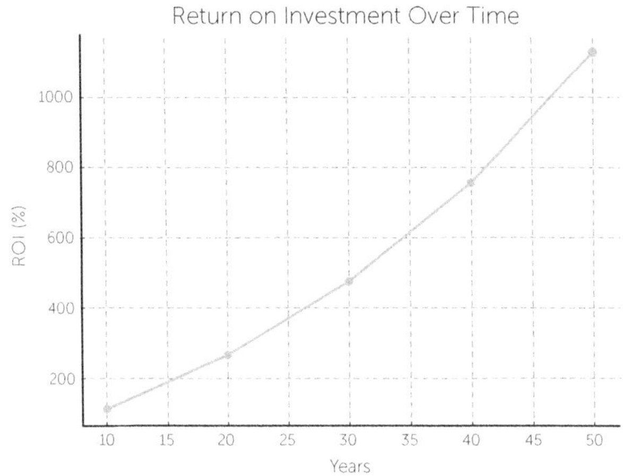

The difference over time is staggering. After the first decade you will have roughly doubled your money.* But wait another forty years and you would have made eleven times your money.† The power of patience is transformational, and our opening chapter explores this further.

* The value of the house increases to $134k, yielding a profit of $34k, an ROI of 115%.

† The value of the house increases to $438k, yielding a profit of $338k, an ROI of 1128% or 11x.

1

Chapter One: Sharks, Elephants & Tortoises

Adopt the pace of nature: her secret is patience.
– Ralph Waldo Emerson

One of the late Stephen Covey's suggested habits was to "begin with the end in mind". Expressed another way, what are we solving for? We have a choice of what type of investor we want to be. The question can be asked in the context of being an individual investor of your own savings, or as an investment fiduciary managing the capital of others. This chapter is written through the lens of an investment manager, but the lessons also apply at the individual level. In preview, what follows is an invitation to be like nature and to build wealth slowly. You may have received more appealing invitations. Bear with me. This is an invitation worth considering.*

There are three broad categories of investment manager.

* If you are introverted, you may greet black-tie dinner or cocktail party invitations with the same enthusiasm as a court summons.

Our first category is the internal rate of return ('IRR') chaser (the sharks) which crave the "IRR Hall of Fame". They want to be known for the highest annual returns, demonstrating their predatory prowess.

The second category is the assets under management ('AUM') maximiser. The AUM maximisers (the elephants) seek the "AUM Hall of Fame". They may profess to solve for high risk-adjusted returns. In practice, incentive-driven revealed preferences show that they more frequently solve for maximum AUM. The seductive economics of earning a percentage fee of gross assets, puts the focus squarely on asset gathering. Turns out marketing is easier than generating differentiated risk-adjusted returns.

There is another approach, however, and that is to act like nature and solve for staying in the game for the longest possible time, i.e. solve for survival (the tortoises). Do this and you may find your way into the "Money Multiple Hall of Fame".*

In the compounding formula, where 'r' is the rate of return:

$$(1 + r)^n$$

'n', otherwise known as the exponent, or the number of years, does a surprising amount of the heavy lifting. If you start with $10,000 and compound at 10% per annum, your money multiple at the end of each subsequent decade is exponential.

Money Multiple on $10,000 earning 10% p.a.	
Decade One	2.6x
Decade Two	6.7x
Decade Three	17.4x
Decade Four	45.3x
Decade Five	117.4x

The benefits of staying in the game for each incremental decade are simply staggering. Very few money managers have multi-decade track records. Simply surviving as a competent investment manager for multiple decades puts one in the rarified company of people like John Templeton, Peter Lynch, Warren Buffett, T. Rowe Price, Joel Tillinghast, Ron Baron, Chuck Akre, and Bill Nygren.

* You invest $1,000 and get back $2,000 for a 2X money multiple. IRRs can be flattered in a way that money multiples can't.

From Entropy to Eternity

Rather than becoming a boring tortoise why not be a shark and solve for the highest returns? Afterall, why get rich slowly when you can do it quickly? The main reason is that being in a hurry to get rich, disproportionately increases the risk of getting dealt out of the game. Expecting to get flush, you get flushed out instead. Navigating investment markets is a delicate and frequently fatal affair. Anything multiplied by zero is zero, no matter how big or strong the anything.

Nature operates on a systematic level, aiming for the long-term survival of the whole, often at the expense of the individual components. Nature is solving for eternity. Crucially it does so in the full knowledge that ongoing major shocks are inevitable. For investors and active managers, the challenge lies in not becoming roadkill on the highway of relentless collective progress. This challenge is daunting due to the natural inclination towards entropy or increasing disorder and decay. Businesses must continuously adapt, safeguard, and enhance themselves to sustain their value and avoid dissolution or acquisition by those more adept at navigating these conditions. Portfolio managers need to be prepared for the future equivalents of the tech bust, the global financial crisis, and COVID-19. Investing is hard.

Movement and adaptation are essential for survival. Even sharks move consistently in an attempt to avoid decay. However, mere activity doesn't ensure safety; not all environments are equally rewarding, especially in the context of the irreversibility of time, where you don't get the chance to undo a prior action. Consider I offer you the following bet. We toss a coin and if it comes up heads, I pay you 50%, if it comes up tails you only lose 40%.* Should you take this bet? The answer seems obvious, of course you should as it has a positive expected profit of 5% of the stake. Despite a positive expected return per toss, the reality of playing over time reveals a different picture. Due to the disproportionate impact of losses, continuous play results in a gradual depletion of wealth, because a loss of 40%, followed by a gain of 50% only gets you back to 90% of your original value, highlighting the *miserable math of mistakes.*† What looks like a good bet in isolation, played over time ultimately results in financial ruin (in circumstances where we are risking the majority of our wealth at each turn. Position sizing matters).

Durable by Design

There is wisdom in the motorsport adage; "to finish first, you must first finish" or as Niki Lauda put it somewhat more cryptically, "the secret is to win going as slow as possible."

Nature is *durable by design.* Enabling characteristics include:

- Self-repair and adaptation.
- Efficiency and resourcefulness.
- Diversity and redundancy.
- Scalability and integration.
- Natural selection/survival of the fittest.

* Mathematician Ole Peters has explored this thought experiment in detail in his work on ergodicity.

† Frequently exacerbated by irrational behaviour after the mistake, the poker equivalent of going on tilt.

Reducing errors, or minimising the impact of errors seems mundane, but, just like in tennis, it is the key to survival. If we want compounding to work its exponential magic, we simply need to make sure we survive long enough. Indeed, if the 'n' is long enough, 'r' doesn't matter so much. A single dollar compounded at 2% annually from the birth date of Jesus would exceed all the wealth in the world today.*

Management teams that emulate nature seek to build businesses that are *durable by design.* Such businesses typically demonstrate:

- A culture of long-term thinking over short-term profit maximisation.
- No/low leverage.
- Large and improving consumer/customer surplus.
- Heightened sensitivity to threats/risks (think Andy Grove's dictum "only the paranoid survive").
- Prioritise flexibility, stability, and optionality over optimisation.
- High returns on capital employed earned through a durable, and preferably widening, competitive advantage.

The Tortoises Diet

If as investors, we are solving for duration, then we need to be thoughtful about our information diet. We should choose the cumulative over the cyclical and the timeless over the topical. More time spent read-

* None of us have that long a timeframe, but the maths are nevertheless instructive, if not downright astonishing.

ing annual reports, less time on daily 'news'. More time studying business models, less time on the latest Model T. More time studying base rates,* less on trying to divine the path of interest rates. More time avoiding arrows, less time chasing rainbows.

Conclusion

Investors can't solve for eternity, but we can design for durability, first and foremost through error minimisation. Error minimisation begets resilience, which, when combined with optionality, most closely resembles nature's relentless productive path.

That said, solving for duration has a price. Compared to the sharks and the elephants, which will at times respectively be famous or visible, the duration seeking tortoise will be neither, spending countless years in obscurity in the investment wilderness (especially in bull markets). The tortoises time in the wilderness will feel undeserved and random, capricious even.

* Base rates are a fundamental probabilistic concept and the cornerstone of Bayesian reasoning. Every prediction should be calibrated in the context of the relevant prevailing base rate.

2

Chapter Two: The Daily Capricious Score

> *Patience is bitter, but its fruit is sweet.*
>
> – Jean-Jacques Rousseau

Over the past three decades, I've invested in both public and private companies and still do, but over time my leaning has skewed in favour of liquid* public companies. There are many reasons for this, but they largely flow from the optionality provided by liquidity.

* What is considered liquid will depend on how much capital you are managing.

- It's easy to increase or reduce the size of one's position in a particular security.
- Fluctuating prices provide a continuous source of free options to either buy or sell a security and critically you don't have to act on any of them. The market offers you thousands of new choices every day. * It's a river of free optionality. You don't have to exercise any, but just a handful of good decisions can make all the difference.
- The options that are free and open to investors are equally open to management teams that can choose to either buy back or issue shares when conditions are compelling, a formidably effective tool when wielded by rational management.
- Being a public company normally puts a particular kind of discipline on management in terms of disclosure, regulations, and shareholder accountability.

These may not look like much, but in practice the optionality of being able to change one's mind, especially in scurrying out of mistakes while minimising losses, is hugely valuable over an investment lifetime. There are times when the market serves you with extraordinary value, but if you are fully invested in private illiquid companies, you can't take advantage of that. If an illiquid company becomes wildly undervalued, you are unlikely to be able to add to your posi-

* Even the fluctuating prices within your existing portfolio is a valuable source of optionality. Firms like the Canadian company Turtle Creek Asset Management have written publicly about how they harvest this volatility.

tion, or if you have made a mistake, it can be like a marriage with no right to divorce.

A liquid public company that can grow intrinsic value by say 10% p.a. over five years on reasonable assumptions, and with a high degree of certainty, is a thing of beauty. The rate of return bar for private company investing should be substantially higher. If your goal is to take the tortoise's road to prosperity there is ample scope to do so through public company investing alone.

But public investing doesn't quite come completely free. Public company investing extracts its own price in what I call the *daily capricious score.* Because public securities are priced daily you get a daily scorecard. And that scorecard can become your identity. Over any short-term timeframe, the score is indistinguishable from random. It is simply capricious, and the public securities investor must live with it. This random score applies not just over days or weeks, the score can be off base for years. Yes, you could have a "score" that for years bears no resemblance to what's really happening with the investment choices you have made. But your Net Asset Value ('NAV') per share is your NAV, and your sense of self can get wrapped up in a warped NAV. And that works multiple ways, you have a high undeserved NAV and hubris takes hold, or you have an undeserved low NAV and despair sets in, or an undeserved low NAV and things are taken from your control.*

How can we deal with the daily capricious score?

* This is related to process versus outcome. A good process can still produce a bad outcome and a bad process can produce a good outcome. Appreciating the roles of luck and skill is core to understanding the essence of investing.

In the end, it is probably down to a combination of our personal temperament and the expectations/structure of the capital we manage. Everyone needs to understand the long-term nature of the journey and the potential for drawdowns along the way. It is fundamental to public securities investing. Understanding this is all fine but I still don't like getting a bad score, deserved or otherwise. I keep a picture of how I looked in the thick of the March 2020 selloff and it's a tad disturbing. I looked terrible and was feeling the stress which may have been exacerbated by the wider uncertainty of COVID and the fact that I was acting as a fiduciary of third-party capital.* For some reason, I was far less phased by the 2008 banking crisis but that may have been because it was just my personal capital back then. March 2020 felt so much tougher. To give you some sense of the 'in the moment' environment, below is an extract of a note that I sent to my investors on 19 March 2020†, incidentally just a few days before the market bottomed:

> "Given the extreme moves in markets, I wanted to provide a brief update on where we sit right now.
>
> I will follow up with a full update at the end of the month.
>
> This is an anxious time, and first & foremost I hope you and your families are, and stay, well.

* I should add that I have wonderful investors who put no pressure or unreasonable expectations on me. My stress was both market-driven and self-inflicted. Equanimity has its limits it seems.

† I didn't want to wait until quarter end as I figured my investors would be wondering about the scope of the carnage.

As of mid-afternoon today our YTD NAV is down approximately 36%.

Since the quarter began, I have been rotating into higher quality companies.

While the markdowns on what we own have been extreme, the stocks I managed to get sold (all our banks, Mohawk, Tyman, and some reductions in Ryanair and DFS) are off 46% since exited.

As of this afternoon, the median stock in the S&P 500 and Russell 3000 is off by 35% to 40%, and for many stocks, there is virtually no bottom. For example, as I type, Marriott is down c. 40% today.

My focus is on:

- Ultimate preservation of capital/avoidance of permanent loss;
- Ensuring we participate fully in the ultimate recovery.

This means owning companies that will survive this crisis and come through the other side in a stronger position.

Given travel restrictions and social distancing I suspect we will defer our next group dinner, but I am happy to chat on the phone or catch up one on one at any stage, either over the next few days or after I report for Q1.

Keep safe and hopefully we get to speak soon.

Thanks,

Lar"

The March 2020 daily scores had enough capriciousness for everyone.

You can decide not to look at the score, or to only do so infrequently, but if you have outside investors the score will find you. And we always need to discern whether the short-term score really is capricious or whether the "wisdom of the crowds" nature of the market has given us a deserved score. When all is said and done, it helps to constantly remind ourselves that it's the capricious score that produces the free optionality that constantly flows from public securities investing. We can't have one without the other.

Before leaving this topic, I should highlight and acknowledge some of the benefits of private company investing. The publicly traded universe is shrinking, and private companies are staying private for longer periods.* They represent an increasing share of economic activity and are a source of diversification. Precisely because privates don't give a daily capricious score, we are less likely to panic and sell at the wrong time. If we hold for longer, that additional duration enables money multiple outcomes, in contrast to IRR outcomes from shorter-term trading. Finance theory suggests that private businesses are riskier and therefore have a higher cost of capital, which should mean higher returns. Also, because we feel losses more severely than we enjoy gains there is emotional value in avoiding the mark-to-market emotional rollercoaster. With private companies we often get more detailed due diligence materials before investing and if

* The incentive to go/remain public in the US is lessened by the compliance and regulatory costs of being a public company, the constant threat of class-action lawsuits, and the increasing availability of deeper pools of capital dedicated to private markets.

we have board representation, we can influence strategy. Another lens of looking at public versus private investing is the ability to keep the costs of mistakes low. For me, I find that easier with public companies as one can exit easily. With privates an influential or majority private shareholder can minimise the cost of mistakes through improving the business, perhaps via new management (an option not available to passive minority holders).

On balance, I personally prefer the flexibility of public securities investing but fully understand the attraction of private markets.*

Conclusion

Public securities investment provides a river of valuable optionality that can be harnessed by individuals, investment managers, and public companies themselves. That free optionality has enormous economic value, but it comes with the emotional cost of the daily capricious score.†

* This is a personal preference. The strategy that works best is the one that you can rationally execute.

† And possibly lower returns from those available in the private markets.

3

Chapter Three: Building Wealth

> *There is only one success...to be able to spend your life in your own way, and not to give others absurd maddening claims upon it.*
> – Christopher Morley

What follows might appear obvious but it's often wise not to overcomplicate things. As someone once said to me, "There is only one cure for baldness and that's hair."

Here are three fundamental components to building wealth.

1. Own things that increase in value.
2. Minimise the impact of mistakes.
3. Minimise other claims on the increase in value.

The first of these is self-evident, the other two should also be, but they often don't get the attention they deserve. They interrupt the natural compounding of the first and it's a cardinal sin (in terms of opportunity cost) to unnecessarily interrupt or dilute the exponential path. It's not just the immediate cost of the error, or other claims on value, it's what that lost value could have compounded to over our investment lifetime. I have a friend who bemoans his "$50,000 mattress" that he bought many years ago, paid for by selling a few thousand dollars' worth of stock options in the company where he worked.*

Own things that increase in value

While traders seek to profit from movements in prices, investors earn their returns by sharing in the profits of an enterprise over time. Those on the patient path understand that time is a fundamental part of the investment equation. Is time our friend or our enemy, and if it is the latter, what can we do about it? Let's go further and restate it more emphatically, I'd hazard that the four most important words in investing are: "Is time our friend?"

* There is possible hindsight bias here. My friend's refrain is only valid if he would have kept that particular stock and kept it through the vicissitudes of the market. The point remains however, compounding should not be interrupted or diluted.

Buffett said that time is the friend of the wonderful business and the enemy of the poor one. Quality is durable. In tough periods, which always occur, better businesses typically emerge disproportionately stronger. A poor business eventually gets in trouble; it is more speculation than investment. The quality business improves over time, and the poor one implodes. The highest quality businesses earn high returns on capital. As investors, it's even better if they have ample capacity to re-invest profits at continued high returns. Time is your friend with such businesses. By contrast, if you purchase an average business that is trading at a discount, even a large discount, to its true value, time is not your friend because the longer it takes for the valuation gap to narrow, the worse your result (in terms of IRR). All else being equal, time favors 'growth' investing (let compounding do the work), over 'value' investing (seeking to close an intrinsic value gap in the shortest possible time). Time spent understanding quality businesses has a long shelf life. If the current valuation is not attractive, the understanding is not wasted as there is a reasonable prospect of it becoming actionable at some point.

It is a big advantage to be able to examine opportunities through a medium to long-term lens. Lengthening the lens applies the focus to the thing that matters most, long-term sustainable earnings power. We frequently forget that a company's earnings over the next few years represent but a small fraction of overall value. We befriend time when we focus on the long term.

Looking at the idea of befriending time from another angle, what if we chose stocks in the same way that we chose our friends? The quality friend, and quality stock, is always getting better, often better than you expected. They are frequently at their best in bad times. When the going gets tough they are growers rather than victims.* A bad friend will drag you down and probably take a disproportionate amount of your time and attention. Having low expectations may help, but this is a lousy way to go through life. (It's interesting to observe how many investors ultimately shift from a 'value' style to a 'quality/growth' style, but rarely do investors move in the opposite direction).

Minimise Mistakes

Mistakes are costly. Consider the following: Two back-to-back years of 30% gains followed by a single 30% loss. What's your total gain? Despite an intuitive sense that two plus thirties and one minus thirty leaves you with one plus 30% gain, that's not how the math works. The above sequence gives a three-year compounded return of under 6%. The tortoise delivering a steady 10% per annum might be quite envious for two of those plus 30% years, but ends up in a better place for having avoided a large draw-down.

While making mistakes might be the surest way to lose money, it is unfortunately not the only way. Virtually nothing is 100% predictable. You can be 95% sure of something and be butchered by the one in twenty occurrence, perhaps fatally if levered. Over time, everyone will get their fair share of chance

* Nature has relevant examples like the Mangrove Tree that can thrive in salt water or the Antarctic Blackfin Icefish which has antifreeze proteins in its blood. Not exactly an analogy for being better in worsening situations, but one of being able to occupy a harsh niche in a way that others can't.

events, good and bad. We acknowledge the role of chance, but we can't change it. So instead, we focus on the things that are in our control, and minimising mistakes is in this category.

The two most common sources of mistakes are:

(a) not knowing what you are doing; and

(b) leverage.

The former speaks for itself but is sometimes forgotten, especially in bull markets. Not knowing what you're doing exposes you to uncompensated risks. So does overestimating your ability. Thinking you are smarter than you are leads to real trouble. Buffett speaks of knowing the edge of one's circle of competence and it's a fundamental skill in error avoidance. I like to think that I have some dots of competence. Occasionally I'll join a few dots and find something safe and interesting to do. Over ninety percent of my problems have come from operating outside my dots of competence.

Relatedly, a valuable characteristic of competence is understanding the nature of the particular issue being tackled. A helpful classification* of issues is to ask whether we are dealing with a 'puzzle', a 'problem' or a 'mess'. Puzzles are the easiest. They can be clearly stated and have a correct answer, like the amount of withholding tax on a dividend. Problems are more complicated. Will a new product be a success? We can make a probabilistic based judgement, but no more. With messes (e.g. company fraud) we don't even know if we are asking the right questions. Contextual competence understands the fundamental characteristics of issues under consideration.

* Popularised by Russell Ackoff.

The topic of leverage is more complicated because when it comes to building wealth, leverage can be wonderful. In itself, leverage is neither good nor bad. It simply magnifies results. In both directions. The type and timing of leverage matters. Bad leverage has one or more of the following features.

- You don't fully see it, for example, hidden operating leverage or some cliff risk dynamics in a business model (related to not knowing what you are doing).
- Shorter in term than the assets that are being financed, either directly, or indirectly through conditions that can trigger demand for repayment or higher costs.
- Expensive.

In building wealth, leverage helps if you are in a hurry; but, if you want to build *and keep* wealth, it doesn't help to be in a hurry. Some leverage is created more equal than other leverage. There are some examples where significant wealth has been built and kept using cheap term leverage. The 'float' in a profitable insurance business is a good example. So is well-located property bought at the right time in the cycle, financed long-term at low fixed rates.

Minimise Other Claims

Three thieves conspire to erode our wealth. These are inflation, expenses, and taxes.* Inflation is the silent thief. The decade from 1973-82 inclusive saw average annual CPI inflation of 8.7% in the US, and peak inflation of 13.3% in 1979. That was simply daylight

* There are others too, including being gazumped in a complex capital structure or from management teams extracting value in nefarious ways.

robbery for savers. Inflation has recently returned from a long absence and is a constant threat to real wealth preservation.

The emergence of a multi-trillion passive investment industry represents retaliation to the thieving power of expenses.

Most investors intuitively understand the performance drag caused by inflation and expenses. When it comes to taxes fewer investors have this intuitive understanding. This is somewhat surprising because tax efficacy is a critical component in compounding wealth. Consider the following two (purely illustrative) scenarios. In Scenario A assume you are a tax-exempt individual (perhaps through a retirement account) directly owning 100% of an Irish-domiciled productive business that is taxed at 12.5%. The business earns €100 in pre-tax profits per year and fully distributes its earnings to you as owner. In this case, you get to keep €87.50 as illustrated below.

Scenario A

For Scenario B assume the company is based in a high tax jurisdiction, paying 40% corporation tax, and you are a high marginal rate taxpayer, paying 50%. The picture in scenario B is not quite as pretty.

Scenario B

While this is a simplified example, it shows the importance of tax efficacy at both the source and tax efficacy in your hands. The difference is enormous.

There are other examples where being alive to hidden tax dynamics is important.

1. Knowing whether dividend or interest withholding tax is deducted from your income-producing securities, and if deducted whether it is recoverable. The taxes may be recoverable, but the administrative task can be cumbersome and costly. In some countries withholding tax can snare a third or more of your income.
2. Share buybacks are preferable to dividends if you are in a high-income tax bracket.
3. Government tax policy can materially impact earnings, a particular risk for resource companies, lotteries, and "sin stocks" like alcohol or tobacco.
4. Companies may report overseas earnings gross of repatriation taxes. The foreign earnings are reported gross, but taxes on repatriation may reduce what's truly available to shareholders.
5. Corporate finance theory* suggests that the value of a company should not be impacted by how leveraged it is. But this ignores the present value of the tax shield provided by interest deductibility.†

* As taught in business schools.
† The wider dangers of leverage remain.

6. While tax exemptions are preferred, tax deferrals are also valuable. The tax deferral is the economic equivalent of an interest-free loan (i.e. good leverage). Over long periods the benefits of tax deferral can be substantial. Think of it as free gearing at the level of the tax that would otherwise have been due.
7. For taxable individuals it is usually better to own long-term compounders. Say you invest €1m in a stock, and it doubles. You sell the stock. Assume 30% capital gains tax. After doubling, you will have €1.7m to reinvest. Let's say the new stock also doubles to €3.4m. You again sell and now pay €0.5m tax (€1.7m @ 30% tax), leaving you with €2.9m to re-invest. If you hadn't sold, you would still have €4m working for you.* For taxable investors, reinvestment candidates have a higher bar than your existing holding.

Conclusion

Wealth is built through owning productive assets, bought at reasonable prices, minimising the cost of errors, and holding onto as much of the fruits of the productive capacity as possible. While building wealth is one thing, keeping it is quite another. What's not kept can't be compounded. The opportunity cost of compounding foregone is enormous.

* Assuming your existing choice matched the returns of the replacement stock.

4

Chapter Four: A Tale of Two Tails

Everyone must choose one of two pains: The pain of discipline or the pain of regret.
– Jim Rohn

Returns from stocks don't follow a normal probability distribution. Professor Hendrik Bessembinder, studying results from 1926-2022, documented that nearly 60 percent of the stocks of U.S. public companies failed to earn returns above Treasury bills. Astoundingly only two percent created more than 90 percent of the total wealth.* This is a distribution that one would more typically associate with venture capital, but it also turns out to be true of the wider stock market. The left tail of the distribution includes an army of bad or mediocre investments

* Well, it's not quite as astounding as some would claim. Given the very long-term timeframe of the Bessembinder study, this is what you would expect, as time kills most companies in the end. Looking over rolling one-, three- or five-year returns would paint a very different picture and the ability to trade around valuations in liquid securities can enable healthy results even deep into the left tail as price volatility is far wider than intrinsic value volatility.

while the right tail has a handful of superstars. Armed with this information, we might categorise investors into one of two types:

Type A: The Right Tail Chasers.

Type B: The Left Tail Avoiders.

Two inter-related approaches are at play here. Firstly, the seek winners or avoid losers framework, and then the degree to which either of those approaches argue for a concentrated or a diversified portfolio. Logically, if you want to do better than average, you must either have better than average winners or fewer than average losers. One could theoretically have both, but in practice maximising winners and minimising losers are distinct disciplines, requiring differing skill sets and modus operandi.

A lot of statistical work has been done on the value of catching the right tail and investment careers have been made off the back of it. Less work has been done on the value of avoiding the left tail. In terms of base rates, avoiding a sufficient* number of the left

* We can't, nor don't need to, avoid it all. Keeping away from the most egregious losers, while owning a diversified portfolio of sensible businesses purchased at reasonable prices, will handily move us along the patient path.

tail looks like an easier path to execute than trying to find the right tail winners (which are far fewer and are mostly only evident in retrospect).

Concentrate or Diversify?

For the purposes of this discussion, I have, somewhat arbitrarily but not unreasonably, assumed that a concentrated portfolio has fewer than twenty positions. In the spirit of inversion, let's firstly highlight the problems with each approach: The main problems with concentration:

1. Mistakes are costly.
2. Bad luck is costly (and emotionally painful).

You don't want to be so concentrated that you are killed by mistakes or bad luck. Time's irreversible arrow means that you never get a chance to let compounding work its magic. Fatal mistakes turn what could have been an infinite game into a once off knock-out competition. There is no comeback kid.

The main problems with diversification:

1. Holdings are not properly understood or monitored carefully enough.
2. It's difficult to materially outperform the market over a sustained period.
3. It's almost impossible to deliver exceptional returns over a long period of time.

What then are the factors which should guide one's approach? My sense is that it depends primarily on two things:

1. Who you are.
2. What you buy (and keep).

1. Who you are.

Investing is a personal/behavioural activity. Whether to concentrate or to diversify should be consistent with one's temperament and confidence levels. Walter Schloss liked to diversify as it helped him sleep more easily. Others diversify as a demonstration of humility and a recognition of fallibility. Charlie Munger preferred to concentrate in those few investments where he had high conviction. He firmly believed that, for knowledgeable investors who know their circle of competence, to do otherwise made no sense. Most, but not all*, of the truly great investment records have been built through concentrated investing. There is clearly some survivorship bias in these records, and I would strongly suggest that there may also be a 'brilliance bias'.

If you took a sample of, say 500 concentrated investors and 500 diversified investors, and looked at their results over a ten-year period, the concentrators would surface a few outstanding track records (which could be luck or skill) but also a lot of wash outs. The diversifiers will have far fewer wash outs.†

Concentrated investing is hard and is probably getting harder as the rate of change in business models accelerates. A concentrated investor must have a strong stomach to withstand the ulcers of underperformance. If you are going to concentrate successfully you need to be emotionally strong and exceptionally smart. Whichever approach you choose, that choice

* Walter Schloss, Peter Lynch and Joel Tillinghast had wonderful long-term track records with highly diversified portfolios, which is a significant and rare achievement.

† This is why elephantine asset gatherers like to diversify, to the point of 'index-hugging'. It's safer in the middle of the herd.

should, as far as possible, preserve your ability to behave rationally, especially at market extremes when rational behaviour is most needed.

2. What you buy (and keep).

This might sound obvious but certain investments are simply not suitable for concentrated investing (if you are solving for survival). Such investments include small cap stocks, leveraged entities (especially in commodity industries), mezzanine debt, correlated holdings (in the business sense), start-ups, concept stocks, options, and basically anything that has a non-negligible chance of going to zero. For concentrated investing to work well, you need to both avoid losers and own/keep winners. Keeping the winners requires a tolerance for volatility as they will frequently represent a very large percentage of your portfolio, and, historically, most right tail outliers have suffered multiple material drawdowns.

In one sense the concentrators and diversifiers are in violent agreement. Both would like to own and keep right tail outliers. It's just that they have a different perspective on how that's done. The right tail chasers feel they have the brilliance to find them, while the diversified left tail avoiders don't have that same confidence, so they cast a wider net.

Conclusion

It's not clear to me whether concentration or diversification are naturally stapled to a specific side of the left/right tail debate. Diversification is a dependable way to garner market returns, but you probably won't do much better than the market.

For those with the ability and equanimity, concentrated investing is a more likely path to material long-term market beating returns.

If one is solving for duration, a diversified left-tail avoidance strategy seems like the appropriate route.

The most important thing is to choose the approach that matches your skills, objectives and temperament, and that the choice is a deliberate one made with an understanding of the relative merits of each approach. If this seems nuanced, that's because in practice it is. We each must choose our sandbox. Choose wisely.

PART II
UNDERSTANDING THE TERRAIN

In Part I we chose the patient path. Now let's get to know the terrain so we can recognise opportunities when they come our way. Some of these chapters are longer as we delve into the domain. We can't even begin to cover everything, but I've tried to include what I feel are some foundational topics, with an emphasis on those areas that are not widely covered in existing investment literature.

We start with the rarified world of structurally advantaged business models.

5

Chapter Five: SABMs – A Collection

> *In general, survival is the only road to riches. Let me say that again: Survival is the only road to riches.*
>
> – Peter Bernstein

Some business models are simply better than others. There is something intrinsic to the nature of the business model itself, that, all else being equal, is a source of advantage. These businesses are durable by design. They have a *Structurally Advantaged Business Model* ('SABM'). To explore this topic in more detail I felt it would be helpful to attempt a classification of SABMs, and to do so in such a way that would make the categories memorable. In this sense it might help with pattern recognition in identifying fertile ground for compelling investments. For example, when Nick Sleep coined the phrase "scale efficiencies shared", he forever seared a rich seam of fruitful situations in his own mind, and in the minds of many others since.

The categories that follow are a mix of the familiar and not so familiar. In some cases, I've done no more than use different language for an existing model, but this can be useful in recall and comparison. My motivation for doing the work here is born from the frustration of watching many of my investments lurch from obstacle to setback, with only the briefest periods of respite. Though the valuations were attractive, i.e., the odds were good, invariably the goods were odd. In the spirit of pursuing a joyful journey, in good company, a question I ask in respect of each potential investment is whether I will look forward to the quarterly conference calls. Most calls come in one of two flavours: results, or stories. The better businesses deliver result after result, the others talk about the weather.

What follows are ten categories of SABM. Each category has advantages that enable durability and high returns on capital employed.*

*I have included current company examples. By the time you are reading this the specific examples may no longer be relevant as capitalism marches along its destructive path, but the principles remain evergreen. Examples from books like *Built to Last* and *Good to Great* illustrate how difficult it is to stay on top for long periods.

SABM #1 – Friendly Financial Leverage

Leverage, in the broadest sense, is fundamental to building anything of scale.* All great business models employ some form of leverage, with scaled distribution (either physical e.g., Coca-Cola and Guinness, or digital e.g., Microsoft) being especially powerful. There is however a small cohort of businesses that derive strength from their liabilities, i.e., from the way in which they are funded.

Insurance float is the classic source of friendly financial leverage. Berkshire Hathaway, Markel Corporation, and Fairfax Financial all benefit from float.

The business model of asset managers is highly leveraged to financial assets under management.

Negative working capital (e.g., supermarkets paid upfront with sixty-to-ninety-day supplier credit), deferred tax, and non-recourse debt (e.g., securitisations) are also sources of friendly financial leverage.

SABM #2 – Critical Non-commoditised Components

This is a business that supplies a critical component, while facing limited competition and, at the same time, it doesn't abuse its position as a critical supplier. The price paid by the purchaser is fair in the scheme of its value chain.

For example, semiconductor manufacturer TSMC supplies leading edge chips to Apple. The cost to Apple is small in the context of its iPhone margins. Until quite recently, TSMC had arguably no competition in leading edge chips, having assiduously built

* We discuss the topic of leverage more fully in Chapter 17.

close to an earned monopoly over decades of extreme customer focus. Other examples include Genus plc which manufactures and distributes genetically enhanced semen for livestock producers, and Chr. Hansen which produces the cultures and enzymes that enable food companies optimise taste, texture, and shelf life.

Suppliers into highly regulated industries where safety is paramount, like pharma and aviation, often find themselves in an attractive duopoly or oligopoly. There is little incentive to purchase relatively inexpensive components in mission critical applications from a second or third tier supplier as the financial saving is minuscule in the context of potential component failure. Costs of failure often go beyond financial loss to loss of life. It would be nuts to skimp on quality.

Holders of scarce or unique resources also fall into the category of non-commoditised critical components.

SABM # 3 – Scale Efficiencies Shared

Articulated by Nick Sleep as 'scale efficiencies shared', this is one of the strongest sources of structural advantage as it is exceptionally hard to compete with. When Jeff Bezos says, "your margin is my opportunity", he is not threatening the small cohort of firms that obsess about delivering extreme customer value.

In the US, Amazon, Walmart, Dominos, Costco, Vanguard, and Southwest Airlines have all pursued strategies of sharing scale benefits with customers, predominantly through lower prices.*

* There are also brand advantages at work here, in terms of the trust built with customers.

European low-cost airlines Ryanair and Wizz Air have pursued similar strategies and in so doing have relentlessly taken market share from traditional airlines.

Microsoft practices a variation of this theme through continually adding valuable features to its office suite without commensurate increases in price. (The next chapter takes a deeper look at software businesses more generally).

The scale efficiencies shared model continually embeds substantial latent pricing power (or consumer surplus) and builds customer loyalty. It's pretty close to a 'win/win' model (except perhaps for pressure put on suppliers).

SABM # 4 – High ROIC Cookie Cutter

The ability and capacity to reliably re-invest free cashflow at a high ROIC* is a wonderful structural advantage.

McDonalds, Dollar General, Walmart, Dominos, Home Depot, Starbucks, and Chipotle are all great US examples of relatively predictable re-investment machines, which some have supercharged by developing a franchising option. Franchisers also get to leverage the growth of their franchisees.

A recent European example is 3i Group plc's investment in the non-food, discount retailer Action. Action's store investments boast an eighteen month pay-back period, and notwithstanding what has been a 50x money multiple for 3i so far, Action is still growing strongly as of 2024.

Companies that are very disciplined acquirers

* Return on Invested Capital

also fit the high ROIC cookie cutter categorisation. Examples include Constellation Software, Danaher, and Roper. Their path may be less predictable than underpenetrated retail rollouts, but their value accretion rests on a similar premise of a strong degree of repeatable re-investment at high returns.

SABM # 5 – User Generated Content

Consider the differences in the content cost structures of Spotify, Netflix, and Facebook.* For Spotify, most of its subscription revenue is paid away in royalties every time a song is played resulting in gross margins in the twenties. Netflix is in a better position as it pays for its content once and can amortise it over a growing subscriber base in perpetuity. Facebook's content is user generated and its gross margins are a mouth-watering 80%.

X, YouTube and Pinterest are all beneficiaries of the power of user generated content (monetised through targeted advertising). Credit card companies enhance their profit margins through selling user generated data as do many loyalty card companies. User generated content can also be leveraged to provide a better customer service proposition. The Progressive Corporation has done this with telematics, enabling it to better price risk and to build a stickier customer base through offering lower insurance rates for safe drivers.

SABM # 6 – "Both Sides Now" (a.k.a. scaled two-sided networks/network effects)

I don't have anything new to add to what is one of the

* As of 2023.

more powerful business models, a scaled, two-sided network. A scaled two-sided network, commonly referred to as a platform, is extremely powerful and typically results in a winner takes all or winner takes most share of the relevant profit pool. Once both sides are scaled, these are brilliant businesses, but the barriers to entry are typically extremely high given the 'chicken & egg' problem of introducing sufficient liquidity and value to the early network members. Visa and Mastercard are the textbook examples. Other scaled two-sided platforms include Google, Facebook, Auto Trader, Uber, Fiverr, Rightmove and Airbnb.

SABM # 7 – "Privileged Perch"

This is quite a broad category that covers businesses that find themselves with limited competition as they are protected through some combination of legal, regulatory, customary, or reputational privileges.

Patents secure a monopoly for a defined period. Testing & certification firms secure a moat by building the 'gold standard', often with regulatory endorsement. Who wants to have their safety equipment certified by a second-rate tester? Moody's Corporation and S&P Global operate within a ratings duopoly in anointing whether bond issuances are investment grade, benefitting from a standards-based moat. The big four accounting firms enjoy a large reputational privilege, even in the face of some major hiccups. Management teams that want to engender trust with their shareholders are more inclined to choose one of the big four.

Ivy League universities and luxury goods companies also fall into the privileged perch category, through combining reputational/brand advantages with federal student loan eligibility and scarcity respectively. Philanthropist Chuck Feeney became a billionaire by building a tax-advantaged duty-free shopping franchise (a fortune he quietly gave away). State and national lotteries enjoy protected positions, as do certain 'last man standing' businesses (tobacco, cement plants, refineries or related businesses where approvals would no longer be forthcoming).

SABM # 8 "Stuck on You" (a.k.a. high switching costs)

Keeping customers is usually more profitable than finding them. Businesses want customers that stick around. Sticky businesses are said to have high switching costs. Barriers to switching can come from deep integration, user training, and communication network effects (as has historically been the case with Bloomberg terminals for example).

Not all switching costs are created equal. Some customers face substantial switching costs because of deep integration and the large cost/risk of replacement, but if pricing is flexed too much (taking advantage of the difficulty of switching) the supplier leaves itself open to being marginalised over time. The better switching barriers are where the product or service delivers so much value that switching makes no sense. As we explore in the next chapter, software as a service ('SaaS') businesses are in a good position to build a sticky customer base as they can leverage customers usage data and patterns to continually enhance the software.

A variation on the 'stuck on you' theme is the razor/razor blade model, pioneered by Gillette.

Nespresso (cheap coffee machines/expensive coffee pods) and HP (cheap printers/expensive ink) have followed the Gillette playbook.

SABM# 9 – Brands

Think of brands like Apple, Visa, Nike, McDonalds and Amazon. Durable brands hold an advantaged place in customers' minds, an advantage that shows up in loyalty and pricing power. Brands help consumers feel good about themselves, an affinity that reduces the cognitive load of decision making. Brands tend to survive down-turns, deter competition and attract high-quality staff. The durability comes from the inordinate amount of time and investment it took to build the brand in the first instance, and a continued focus on preservation so that customers ongoing trust in the brand is deserved and maintained.

SABM# 10 – Ecosystem Enablers (a.k.a. "win-win")

A lot of the original/historical thinking on moats and valuable businesses has focussed on building advantages that a business can use against its customers through maximising pricing power.

In an age of increasing transparency, the more powerful (i.e., sustainable) models are the ones that are both financially and morally defensible. Such businesses are genuinely win/win in that they support and enable a growing ecosystem. The value they extract from the ecosystem is a mere fraction of the value they enable (perhaps 5% or less).

Microsoft is a good example of an ecosystem enabler.

Conclusion

The above taxonomy of SABMs should cover most of the valuable waterfront. A great business model can be benchmarked against the degree to which it fits one, or, more likely, a few, of the ten categories outlined.

SABMs are a special category of business. All else being equal we should be willing to pay more for a SABM. They fit the patient compounder's philosophy of seeking safe longevity. They are all long optionality and are more likely to be one of those rare businesses that find their way into the right tail of outperformers. Who wouldn't like to own a few of those?

As I was exploring the range of SABM's with colleagues, some suggested that software businesses fitted the profile. I concluded that the category is too broad to qualify as there is a lot of variability across the software industry and disruption is rife. That said, the software industry has many advantages which we will examine in the next chapter.

6

Chapter Six: Saas - Exploring What Matters

It is not the employer who pays the wages. Employers only handle the money. It is the customer who pays the wages.

– Henry Ford

Software businesses have many attractive features. These include low capital requirements and the ability to rapidly scale with a minimal marginal cost of distribution. The price point is frequently low in the context of the value to customers. Software businesses have therefore been, and continue to be, a fruitful sector for investors. The combination of modest capital needs and non-linear scaling potential is potent. That said, not all software business are SABM's. Barriers to entry are low, technologies change rapidly, and disruption is rife. The rest of this chapter looks at some of the characterises that we should be interested in when looking to understand or invest in a software business.

Anyone starting a software business today is highly likely to do so in a Software-as-a-Service ('SaaS') framework, while established software firms are rapidly transitioning from a product/up-front licence model to a SaaS model. Why is this? It's obvious you might say: It's because SaaS is a better business model. Indeed. I would just add a follow up question; better for whom? Done well, a SaaS business can be superior for all stakeholders, including customers, the software provider, and its equity owners.* The best business models ensure that everyone in the ecosystem is a beneficiary of continuous progress. Let's explore that a little further.

SaaS Done Well

The SaaS customer wants:

1. Software that is fit for purpose, stable, secure, and intuitive.
2. Seamless updates to the latest version.
3. Extreme value for money (i.e. a large consumer surplus), or at the very least transparent pricing that is fair/proportionate to value derived/usage.
4. To share in the progress/economies of the software supplier (features, learning,

* I have a personal investment in Snapfix, a private SaaS company that was founded by a friend of mine. It has been instructive to witness the progression from just an idea to a firm that is now serving businesses across the globe.

use cases etc.). There is alignment and participation in the compounding utility of the product over time.

5. To be able to easily switch suppliers if unhappy with the product or service.

The purpose of business is to profitably create and service a satisfied customer. It therefore follows that the software provider (and, by definition, its equity holders) should strive to give customers what they need. Numbers 1 & 2 above are table stakes. Smarter, long-term oriented SaaS companies deliver on numbers 3 & 4 as well. But they are doing so to make 5 less likely. And that's fine if the customer is sticky because the product is excellent, and the SaaS provider is still delivering extreme value for money. But if the SaaS provider abuses (either through pricing or lack of product development/support) a sticky customer relationship, then trust breaks down and competition will eventually work its way into the cracks.

If I'm building a SaaS business for the future, or investing in one, I would strive to deliver on 1 to 4 above, but I would also want the relationship to be very sticky, and yet, would not seek to abuse that stickiness in any way. There are many reasons not to exploit customer stickiness:

- Your customers become your advocate reducing new customer acquisition costs.
- Your business is more robust against competitive threats.
- In an increasingly open and transparent world, trust-based relationships are the only ones that will endure.

In a sense we can think about a customer stickiness continuum which distinguishes between good, bad, and neutral degrees of lock-in. The categorisations may not be perfect, but I'll hazard a guess that such a continuum looks broadly as follows:

SaaS: Customer Stickiness Continuum
(from the perspective of the customer)

Good Lock-in	Bad Lock-in	Neutral Lock-in
• High customer surplus (i.e. great ROI) • Product utility gets better with use/over time • User competence improves with use	• Long term contracts • Deliberately technically difficult/ awkward to switch • Abusive monopoly suppliers	• Client integrates the software with other systems (though this can turn to bad lock-in if abused by the SaaS vendor)

There are other useful things a SaaS provider can do, many of which are not possible outside a SaaS framework, which is what makes SaaS such an effective business model.

1. **Pricing flexibility.** Because software usage is measurable in real time, the SaaS provider can design pricing that is more attuned to the value derived, or the perceived value derived by the customer.
2. **Upsell identification.** Highly engaged users are easily identified, as are usage patterns that indicate upsell or product development opportunities.
3. **Managing churn.** Usage visibility allows the SaaS provider respond to low/stopped usage

to proactively find out why, instead of seeing that customer churn away.

4. **Ecosystem Enhancement.** Visibility on effective usage facilitates product improvements that benefit the entire user base.

Investor Perspective

A long-term oriented investor in SaaS businesses should be interested in seeing:

- A clear articulation of the business model.
- A healthy dynamic in the classic lifetime value ('LTV') to customer acquisition cost ('CAC') dynamic. This is not always easy to measure and often leads to over investment in CAC against an LTV that never materialises.
- Relatedly, a steady, or preferably declining CAC.
- A customer centric/product excellence ethos which manifests in upsell opportunities (and therefore a high net dollar retention).
- A dedicated business function that is maniacally focused on customer success (i.e. ensuring customers actual use of the product delivers compelling value for them).

Conclusion

For many businesses, once their product is shipped, they have limited understanding of how it is experienced by the customer. SaaS models are different. The defining benefit of the SaaS business model is its real-time ability, through visibility of how customers use the product, to service its customers particularly well. When that's the case, everyone wins.

7

Chapter Seven: Kicking Ass (et Managers) – The Alt Age

> *The constant lesson of history is the dominant role played by surprise. Just when we are most comfortable with an environment and come to believe we finally understand it, the ground shifts under our feet.*
>
> – Peter Bernstein

I could have extended the title of this chapter to "Kicking Ass (et Managers) and other double entendres." In preview, alternative asset management* is a kick-ass industry, and, at the same time, every asset manager gets an occasional good kicking. That kicking can come from several places:

1. Broad-based market declines.
2. Natural "periods in the wilderness" when your portfolio is out of sync with whatever is working in the market.
3. Being wrong.

The kicking† is a "feature not a bug" and is the membership fee to work in an industry that is heavily skewed to the upside.

* As distinct from traditional asset management and hedge funds which were historically attractive but have more recently been somewhat challenged.
† All track records, including the great ones, come with painful intermissions.

So much to like

Who wouldn't like to own and operate a business that:

- Has high returns on capital employed.
- Requires negligible capital to grow.
- Has no bad debts.
- Has minimal operational, logistical, supply chain, manufacturing, or other messy "real-world" challenges.
- In the case of private equity, enjoys the positive asymmetry of exposure to a basket of independently leveraged upside call options.
- Employs professionals that are generally highly engaged and tend to stick around. The industry is attractive to intellectually curious people and is a highly "gamified" performance derby. The high challenge, high reward environment allows firms to build a "competitively advantaged human capital franchise."*

* ValueAct describing its investment in KKR.

- At the industry level, earns an ad-valorem tax on cumulative collective wealth, the ultimate long-term growth industry, as it broadly captures global productive capacity which continually marches forward. The structural leverage of earning a percentage fee on other people's accumulated wealth is enormous.
- For large parts of the industry, predominantly the alternative asset managers, the threat of technological/ structural shifts is far less stark than in other industries.
- Operates in a broadly attractive pricing landscape, at least for the alternative asset managers, in the sense that institutional allocators have accepted that you need to pay for performance/access.
- Has private fund draw-down structures with embedded free optionality as return hurdles are only benchmarked against drawn capital, preserving the free optionality of allocating dry powder to act opportunistically.

Peculiar characteristics

The broader asset management industry has some peculiar characteristics.

- There are areas within asset management, such as low-turnover concentrated equity investing, where an amateur can copy an expert and get close to the same results. I know of no other skill-based profession where someone can so readily emulate an expert.

- More books are written about successful investors/investing than most other professions (except perhaps business or sport). Why are there so few books written about the world's greatest tax consultants, surgeons, or scientists; professions that arguably require greater skill than that of investing? Perhaps it's the unique emulation potential, or more likely our general fascination with outsized wealth accumulation.
- A solo operator or small team can enjoy extraordinary personal economics. Numerous solo individuals manage hundreds of millions. They earn millions per annum in base fees alone,* a remuneration level that is normally associated with the CEO of a large complex organisation. Growth in AUM comes with virtually no additional costs, i.e. close to 100% incremental margins.
- Despite earning a small fortune, most participants don't deliver real value† against an indexing alternative which is close to free. Meanwhile the industry uses the power of story‡ to obfuscate its relative ineptitude.

* Performance fees can add a life-changing kicker.

† Gambling and weight loss companies arguably also fall into this category in that, over time, most gambling customers lose, and most weight loss customers don't lose! (Perhaps the latest arrival of weight loss drugs will break the mould).

‡ See Chapter 16 for more on the power of story.

- The well-founded theory that most people can't beat markets doesn't stop numerous people trying. Call it the "trial versus theory gap", which seems especially wide in this industry.
- It takes at least ten years for anyone to figure out whether results are due to luck or skill, and even then, it's never 100% skill. You probably had to survive cycles, including environments which didn't suit your investment style.

Those who run/own asset management firms understand how good the asset management industry is, yet (for behavioural, mandate driven and some other non-economic reasons) in their portfolio construction they are routinely underweight the sector or have no exposure at all.

Why work anywhere else?

In many things, the choice of game is the defining decision. Deciding where to work is no different. Marshall McLuhan, speaking about the nature of media, famously coined the phrase "the medium is the message" where the form of media communication impacts the message. In choosing a career I suggest that "the median is the message." If you can go into an area where the median result is attractive, the odds are good that you will do ok.* Median compensation within the asset management industry is very attractive, and while it's hard to find reliable median data by industry, it is interesting to

* This is less true with averages, the average may be attractive, but outliers skew the results. If you are going to work where outliers skew the averages, you want to make sure you get multiple shots on goal.

look at the market capitalisation per employee of some of the large alternative asset managers* set in the context of what are already some of the most profitable businesses ever created.

Market Capitalisation per Employee - $M	
Alphabet	8.3
Apple	17.1
Microsoft Corporation	9.0
Visa	19.5
Apollo Global	15.0
Blackstone	18.2
The Carlyle Group	6.5
KKR & Co.	13.7
S&P 500 Median	**1.5**

Data as of 29 August 2022

If you want to find many of the richest people in the world, look within the alternative asset management industry.

Investing in Alternative Asset Managers

For investors who are happy to purchase shares in asset managers, what should we be looking for? Unsurprisingly, given the simplicity and elegance of the asset management business model, three key metrics drive most of the analysis/value:

- AUM
- Fee rates
- Operating margins

At a broad industry level, there is a dichotomy between

*The focus here is on alternative investment management, but other asset management franchises, such as those run by Marriott or Hilton are also attractive business models.

traditional and alternative asset managers across those three key metrics. At one end of the spectrum, large cap listed public equity active asset managers face AUM flow and fee/margin pressures and at the other end the diversified alternative managers are growing AUM while holding fees and margins firm.

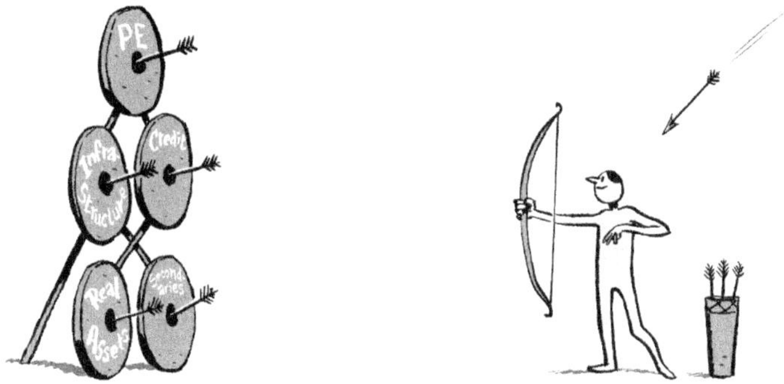

Better Businesses

The better investment management firms are those that:

- Have long duration capital. Many of the alternative asset managers have substantial amounts of "perpetual" capital.* This provides utility like earnings visibility. Or their customers are themselves growing, e.g., pension plans with monthly contributions, providing a dependable source of growth.
- Are scaled institutions that can offer a full suite of investment solutions to the larger capital allocators who are consolidating their limited partner ('LP') relationships. The bigger firms get better access to financing

* What the industry defines as 'perpetual' is not truly evergreen, but in practice should last a decade or more.

and better terms. They face less competition in the larger deals,* and they benefit from an asset management consultancy industry† where the incentives conspire towards recommending the largest players/most recognised brands. There is also a FOMO element with LP allocations, in that if they don't consistently allocate, they may be locked out of future opportunities.

- Can invest across the capital structure thereby enabling them to provide a comprehensive financing solution in a single offering (which may later be syndicated for additional capital markets fees).
- Run multiple strategies over multiple vintages providing performance diversification such that earnings and future growth prospects are not reliant on any single strategy or vintage.
- Have a diverse client base by type and by geography which is important to stability of AUM and therefore fee income.
- Pursue investment strategies that are skill based and have a large "access" component to them, i.e., if you want exposure to the asset class there is heavy lifting involved and it's not simply a case of purchasing a listed equity or a bond with an ISIN. With private assets there is no credible index alternative. Unlike public equities, it's expensive to build an origination platform at scale, leaving the

* Only a handful of firms can write a multi-billion-dollar cheque.
†The classic "friendly middleman" situation.

scaled managers in a strong position. Private assets have the added benefit of lower 'reported' volatility giving investors some psychological comfort to stay the course.*

- Treat investors and limited partners fairly and are super protective of their reputation and culture.
- Have transparent staff compensation systems that are not egregious. A recent trend to allocate most performance fees to staff is a negative here and has stemmed from the fact that public markets have not been willing to put a fair value on volatile performance fees, so the alts management teams have self-servingly said, "ok if the markets won't value them, we will keep them."
- Deliver excess returns per unit of risk, or performance that is at least better than average in enough strategies to enable follow on funds.
- Demonstrate intellectual honesty in performance reporting (an area where the industry has come under fire, especially around IRRs versus money multiples on committed capital, and levered versus unlevered benchmarks).

Once we find asset management firms with those features, we always need to then ask what's priced in, as overpaying is a classic unforced error.

What could go wrong? Some big risks are lurking in the background.

* I appreciate that this is arguably illogical but it's nevertheless true. Cliff Asness wryly calls it 'volatility laundering'.

The first is reputation. An asset management firm can destroy its franchise with bad behaviour. There are plenty examples of firms putting their own interests over those of their clients. This is cynical, deceitful and an unacceptable breach of fiduciary duty. It's also not very smart, a short-sighted killing of "the golden goose."

The second is the degree to which financial assets suffer a material correction. The whole asset management industry has been a huge beneficiary of falling rates and accommodative monetary policy. Asset managers are leveraged to financial markets, and no matter how good they are, their valuations suffer disproportionately during market downturns (even when they have substantial dry powder to invest through the downturn).

The third is founder/key leadership transition. Most of the alternative asset managers have been founded around strong personalities that are synonymous with the firm. Again, it seems like the larger firms may have an advantage here and some have already made the transition, but others have struggled.

Fourthly, the industry has attracted a lot of capital. Too much capital can destroy returns, though the industry has been pretty adept at increasing the opportunity set. Let's face it, the investible universe is enormous. The Alts have been taking share from banks and insurance companies.

Lastly, the compliance and political environment could get much more hostile towards an industry that has massively benefitted from the 'great financialisaton' over the last two decades. We have seen recent examples in the UK wealth management industry where regulators have intervened to protect client interests at significant financial and reputational costs to some of the largest wealth management firms.

Conclusion

Not all asset managers are created equal. While traditional managers are facing pressures on multiple fronts, the scaled diversified alternative asset management world is a structurally advantaged industry. Welcome to "The Alt Age."

If you work in this industry, it's worth pausing to reflect whether you may have been rewarded for simply being lucky,* and confusing that luck for brilliance. Lucky to work in an endlessly fascinating industry, with outsized economics.

For public market investors there is an ever-increasing listed alternative asset manager universe. Look for those that are scaled, diverse, with long-dated capital, run by management that is protective of its reputation and respectful of its clients.

* For example, how many investment portfolios were bailed out from money-printing immediately post COVID?

8

Chapter Eight: The Nature of Cash

It takes character to sit there with all that cash and to do nothing. I didn't get to where I am by going after mediocre opportunities.
– Charlie Munger

Let's turn our attention to the nature of cash which, in a sense is the 'bridge' asset. It's likely the thing we will be parting with in exchange for investments, so it's important to understand what we are giving up.

When reading this chapter, be aware that a fund manager and an individual investor will have different contexts. For most fund managers, their job is to be fully invested. Those who have given them capital will have done so as part of their equity allocation while retaining their own cash or low-risk assets elsewhere. For fund managers with the flexibility to hold cash, the nature of their investment portfolio also has a bearing. A portfolio filled with cash-rich companies with strong balance sheets is different from a portfolio of leveraged companies. The type of portfolio you own will have a bearing on how much cash you hold directly. Please forgive the crosscurrents here, but that's the nuanced reality.*

Let's consider; (i) the nature of cash, and (ii) its place in an investment portfolio.

When we talk about cash, we are talking about a deposit with a financial institution and our exploration might more appropriately be labelled as the nature of money. Cash (in the form of coins and banknotes) represents a small fraction of the total money supply. The majority of what we call money is deposits held with financial institutions.†

The Nature of Cash/Money

The classic definition of money might be as represented by the following diagram. Money is considered sound if it acts as a medium of exchange, a unit of account and a store of value.

The Three Pillars of Sound Money

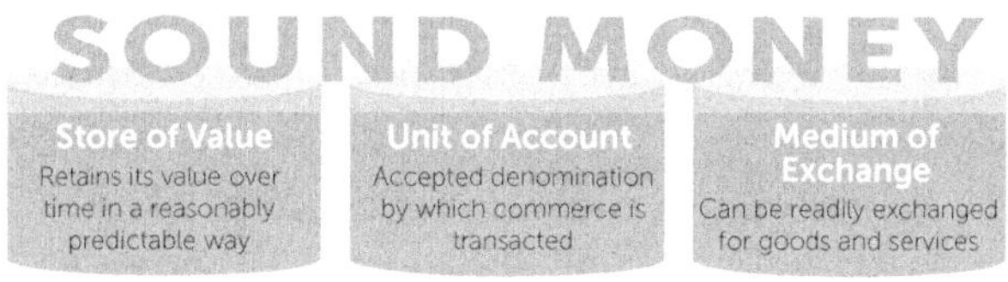

Money is not wealth but rather a claim on wealth. Ultimately money can be exchanged for goods and services, or it can be used to buy productive capacity. If money couldn't be traded for goods or services, or purchase productive capacity, it would have no utility. Money is, in essence, a deferred claim on

* Anything that can be put in a nutshell belongs there.
† Short-term government bonds are 'cash equivalents' that typically deliver better returns than cash held in a current account, providing some offset to inflation.

productive capacity (e.g. the laying hen or the breeding stock) or on the fruits of productive capacity (e.g. the eggs). Productive capacity is the means to deliver the goods and services that people want. Broadly speaking, productive capacity is increasing over time and normally it is better (from a long-term wealth accumulation perspective) to own productive capacity today than; (a) to consume today, or (b) to hold money for future consumption, or (c) to purchase productive capacity in the future. The problem with holding money for a long period of time is that cracks can, and do, appear in the three pillars, especially in money's property as a store of value. The schematic below may help illustrate this dynamic.

Money as a Claim on Productive Capacity

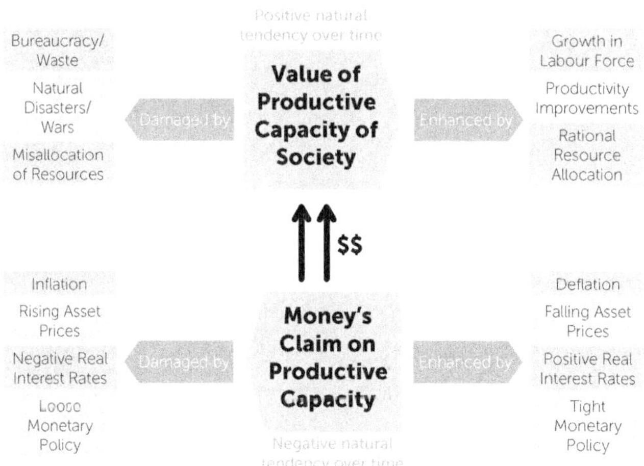

While there are many factors at play, over the medium to long term, productive capacity tends to increase in value in money terms and money has a tendency to decrease in value in units of productive capacity.

Normally, if you have a long-term time horizon and you have sufficient liquid resources for current needs/ possible emergencies, wealth is maximised through owning productive capacity, and not through holding cash.

Cash in a Portfolio Context

Why would a portfolio manager hold cash given the likely longer-term losing proposition (versus owning productive capacity)? There are two lines of reasoning. One relates to what is essentially a timing call. We can think of cash as being akin to a variable claim on productive capacity and there will be times when that claim is more useful than others. The other reason for holding cash relates to the intrinsic optionality of cash. Dealing with the variable claim first and building on our earlier schematic, there are times when it makes sense to hold more cash than normal, for example, if asset prices are very expensive and cash/currency is not being inflated away or debased through excessive money printing (i.e. its properties as a store of value are sound).*

* Cash and short-term government bonds are more attractive when real deposit/interest rates are high.

The Cash Conundrum

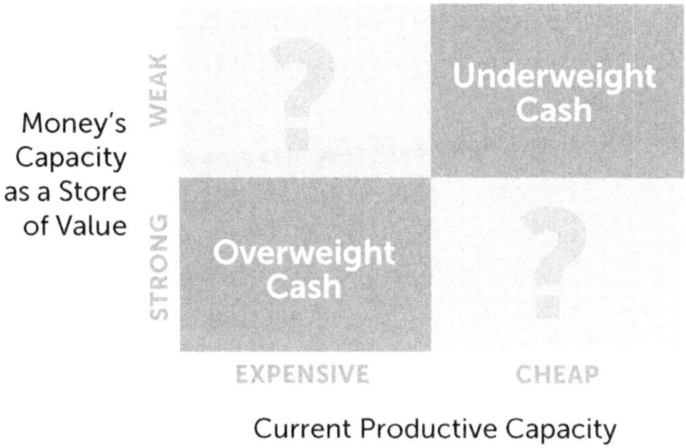

Aside from the timing call there are intrinsic reasons to hold some cash (once combined with a preparedness to hold no cash, or even to borrow, when the circumstances support full investment):

1. *Optionality.* Holding cash is a call option on future opportunity. Time has a habit of occasionally offering up exceptional opportunities and we only need a few to be able to capitalise on them. When the odds are especially favourable, having discipline and recognising such favourable odds is not enough, we must also have both the fortitude and liquidity* to act. We could use hedges instead, but they have cost and execution issues.

* This gets back to my preference for listed liquid securities as discussed in Chapter 2. If you don't have cash but are fully invested in liquid securities, you can still judiciously rebalance existing liquid holdings, profiting from wider than typical value dispersion.

2. *Resilience & Risk Management.* First and foremost, cash enables resilience. History is littered with nasty surprises. Cash is insurance. Insurance is survival. Survival is essential.

   There's a related risk management benefit. Let's say for the sake of simplicity that one could be 100% invested and earn a 6% market return or be 50% invested and earn 12% on the invested portion and nothing on the un-invested portion. Without getting into the weeds of the relative riskiness of the 6% or 12% investments (the 12% investment may in fact be less risky more often than people suspect), we should consider the 50% invested portfolio safer than the 100% invested portfolio. Barbelled portfolios with a mix of safe and risky assets are a durable combination.

3. *Loss Asymmetry.* Feeling the need to be always fully invested increases the risk of overpaying. Recovering the loss associated with overpaying for an asset is not directly proportional to the gain required to recover the loss. A 25% loss requires a 33% gain to get back to even. A 50% loss requires a doubling to break even. Again, we encounter the miserable math of mistakes. You will re-read this refrain multiple times throughout this book as I've unfortunately had to re-learn it multiple times.

4. *Behavioural.* For some portfolio managers, holding higher than theoretically optimal cash levels allows them to stay rational and suits their personality. It may be a conservative bent or a sense that they only want to invest when opportunities are most compelling. I've seen some managers deliver excellent returns notwithstanding a high cash drag and that's impressive. What is less well known is that occasionally those same managers may allow you to invest in a separate account with them that's continually fully invested. If their main fund is good, the managed account may be even better.* In a sense, the managed account holder gets a free ride from the psychological safety of the cash held in the main fund.

Conclusion

Cash is a source of resilience and optionality, but those properties need to be weighed against the opportunity cost of owning productive assets at reasonable prices, which in the long run is the safest way to build wealth.

* This is not universally the case. It's most likely when cash levels are relatively stable.

9

Chapter Nine: The Nature of Options

Don't play cat and mouse games if you are the mouse.
– Johann Rupert, Chairman of Richemont

We talk a lot in everyday life about understanding our options, maximising our options, or keeping our options open. The worst (investment) fate for an investor or trader is to wipe out their capital. Staying in the game is critical, and an understanding of the nature of options is important to avoiding permanent loss of capital. Options are a complex topic. What follows is an exploration of the general nature of options (beyond the niche world of traded options).* Examining investment decisions through an 'options lens' can help us become more rational and thoughtful investors. The

* Those can be fun (and dangerous). During the 2008 St Patrick's weekend I was on holiday with my wife and young kids in Disneyland Paris. In the prior week I had speculatively bought put options on Bear Sterns and the stock dutifully tanked while I was away. I was scrambling to find an internet café to close out the trade, which I did. The profitable trade paid for the trip, but I was clearly not on holiday with my family.

figure below outlines the key features to understand in assessing options.

Options: Key Features

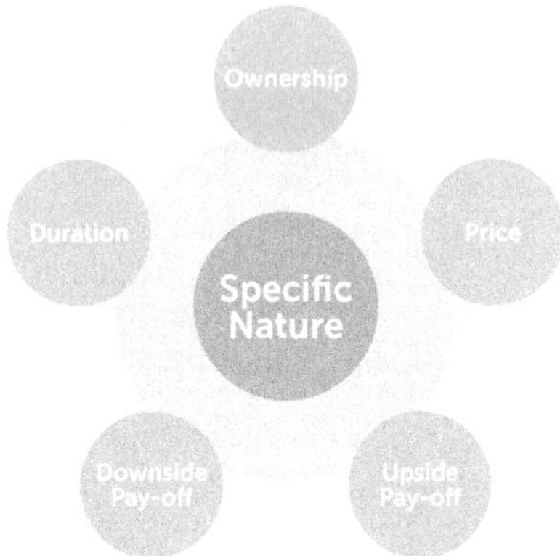

1. Specific Nature. To what exactly does the option relate? The option must relate to something specific. In some cases, this will be quite clear, e.g. the right to buy shares in Microsoft that are listed on a specified stock exchange. But what if someone gave you a gift of a call option on oil? To understand what you own, we need to be much more precise. Is it on West Texas or Brent? Does the option relate to physical oil (where we might have to take physical delivery) or does it relate to a financial contract? If it is a financial contract, can it be net-settled? We also need to understand the fundamental nature. Is it a right to buy (a call), to sell (a put), to extend, or to exchange etc.?

2. Who Owns the Option? The owner of the option (the buyer) is the party that is in control, and the one who gets to make the decision on whether to exercise. The option giver (the seller, or in 'options speak' called the 'writer') is a passive bystander (though the option writer can manage their exposure through hedging).

3. What is the Duration? The duration is the period during which the option can be exercised by its owner.* All else being equal, option owners prefer long duration and option givers (writers) prefer short duration. You want to be in a situation where time is your friend.

4. What is the Option Price? The option price (premium) can be explicit and negotiated up-front (e.g. exchange traded options) or may be embedded and not precisely quantifiable where there is some optionality as part of a wider transaction (e.g. the right to prepay a fixed rate US home loan without penalty).

5. What is the Downside Pay-off Profile? Understanding the downside potential pay-off profile is critical. Never assume that some rare event will never happen. Extreme events happen more frequently than we think or wish. Is the downside known (e.g. buying an equity put or an equity call, where the downside equals the premium paid), capped (e.g. selling an equity put or selling an equity covered call) or potentially unlimited (e.g. selling/writing an un-covered equity call)?

6. What is the Upside Pay-off Profile? Is upside fixed (e.g. selling an equity put or an equity call), capped (e.g. buying an equity put), or unlimited (e.g. buying an equity call).

* Note that traded European and American options have different time windows. European options can only be exercised on a specific date, while American ones can be exercised at any time up to and including a specific date.

Once we understand the nature of an option, we can get a basic sense of what an option's value continuum might look like:

Options Value Continuum

Valuable Option Characteristics	**Dangerous Option Characteristics**
- Uncapped upside - Option bought - Fixed and low/no-cost downside	- Fixed and low upside - Option sold - Uncapped downside
Valuable Option Examples	**Dangerous Options Examples**
- Employee Incentive Stock Grants - High quality, un-levered business franchise bought at a fair or a low price - Lifelong learning - Holding cash ahead of a period of market dislocation	- Selling poorly priced long dated catastrophe insurance - Mezzanine lending to highly levered businesses - Playing multiple games of Russian roulette for small (or indeed large) rewards

To explore this further let's use an options lens to compare three different activities: lending, writing catastrophe insurance and buying equities.

	Lending	Writing Cat Insurance	Buying Equities
Downside	*Capped at the Loan Amount*	*Uncapped (unless re-isured or a specific cap is contracted)*	*Capped at the Investment Amount*
Upside	*Capped*	*Fixed*	*Unlimited*
Nature	*Selling a Put*	*Selling an uncovered call*	*Buying a call*

The phrase 'picking up pennies in front of a steamroller' has been used to describe banking and insurance. The analogy is harsh but true. Lending without prepayment penalties can look especially poor under an options lens. If things are going well for the borrower the lender gets repaid early, earning minimal income. If things go badly a 100% loss is a possibility. This is poor asymmetry.

Options Checklist

When making investments or financial decisions it is instructive to consider them through an options lens. Questions we might ask include:

1. What explicit options are we buying or selling?
2. What implicit options are we buying or selling?
3. What is the shape of the pay-off profile?
4. Does the investment have traded options and if so, do they offer either useful information or a more effective way to take/manage exposure?
5. Is our overall portfolio construction (including cash allocations) conducive to capitalising on periods of market dislocation?*
6. Overarchingly, we need to examine the price. We are looking for mis-priced options. Some options are not immediately intuitive but remain valuable. For example, trading a known cost against a future potential regret.†

* Ideally our individual portfolio companies will have the cash and/or access to capital markets and the ability to profit in times of distress. Then we can be fully invested, and the portfolio companies will do the hard work in the hard times. When the going gets tough, the tough get going.

† You know what's expensive? Divorce, divorce is expensive. You know what's cheap? Flowers, flowers are cheap.

Though the above discussion is focused on investing, many of the lessons resonate with how to get the most from life more widely. The adage "don't burn your bridges" is a wise one. Cultivating deserved high-quality relationships and friendships is a valuable options strategy.

Conclusion

In aggregate, we want to construct our portfolio in a manner that combines resilience and upside optionality.

When we look at businesses and management teams, we can learn a lot by considering how they fare under an options framework. Closely examine how management conducts business through an options lens.* Good businesses are long multiple unlimited upside call options which we turn to in the next chapter. Competent management teams understand both the explicit and implicit options they are getting and giving.

Businesses to be wary of are option sellers with poor asymmetry. This is often found in banks and insurance companies where growth can be accelerated by writing expensive options. These negative options are unseen until it's too late, as investors in AIG learned the hard way in September 2008.

Bloomberg columnist, Matt Levine has an apt quote to end here: "It is sometimes useful to think that the shareholders of a bank are not its owners; they are just renting it from its creditors."

* I was recently smiling as I read the 2023 annual report of a maritime transportation company where they (as lessee and option owner) had leased a vessel with two independent two-year extension options, plus a purchase option.

10

Chapter Ten: Option Builders

Now, water can flow or it can crash. Be water my friend.

– Bruce Lee

Having considered the nature of options in the previous chapter it's interesting to think some more about business models that have positive embedded optionality.

An example from earlier is the business of running a private equity asset manager. Each portfolio company is independently leveraged, meaning that if one fails, it doesn't affect the outcome of the others. The winners take care of everything. It's not by accident that carry-eligible* private equity professionals are consistently among the highest paid professionals. In fact, the private equity industry is prolific in minting billionaires. If you are lucky enough to be a carry-eligible partner in a large PE firm, you are wielding

*Private equity firms earn a 'carried interest', which is a profit share on successful exits, typically calculated as c. 15% to 20% of profits provided a specific return hurdle is met. Participating professionals are said to be 'carry-eligible'.

the classic Archimedes long lever.

The venture capital industry is a variation on the same theme. The equity in each investment is a call option on the success of venture backed businesses. The multiple options held by the VC firm stand in stark contrast to those held by the individual CEOs of any given portfolio company. For the VC firm, the startup is one of many things, for the founder it's everything.*

A strong balance sheet is a common factor among option builders. The best opportunities frequently present themselves in times of crisis, when liquidity and confidence are in short supply. Option builders have the dry powder, liquidity, or access to capital markets, to capitalise. They have the resilience to stay the course and extract the time value of options.

Flexible and resourceful teams are a critical, perhaps the critical, underappreciated source of both

* Founder pooling solutions are emerging as a hedge for individual founders where they contribute a percentage of their equity in return for a stake in a founders' collective (and therefore get a better shot at catching a right tail outcome).

option building capacity, and execution, as ultimately the value of option building derives from those that are exercised. Complex options require adept execution skills. Consider the relative contribution between A players and B players. In a classic 80/20 situation, where 20% of your staff (the A team) is delivering 80% of your results, the A team is 16x more effective than the B team. If it's a 90/10 situation, which is frequently the case, the difference is a staggering 81x. As a value-oriented investor, I have frequently underestimated the ability of a great management team to deliver performance that was nowhere to be seen on a spreadsheet or financial forecast.

An 'option-friendly' workforce is likely to be split into many autonomous units, which maximises optionality. For example, Constellation Software has numerous independently run business units. While they share best practices, each unit head has broad autonomy. It may look like a conglomerate, but the DNA is entirely option oriented.

TAM Busters

Firms that continually build options frequently turn into TAM busters. What's a TAM buster? A TAM buster is a business that repeatedly expands its total addressable market. Amazon is probably the poster child, first with its move from books to other categories, then from selling its own goods to creating a third-party seller marketplace and most impressively, the creation of Amazon Web Services. While the first of those TAM busting moves might have been predictable, the others were far less obvious. Blackstone came from nowhere in managing real estate to becoming one of the world's largest property asset managers, breaking out from its core private equity business. Apollo Global has done the same in the US retirement savings market.

Alphabet and Facebook have each busted out of their original target markets, multiple times. The Collison brothers at Stripe are TAM busters, breaking out from payments to a whole host of online business management solutions. Elon Musk knows no borders having re-invented several industries. Daniel Ek at Spotify is going beyond music streaming to break into audio and in so doing has an opportunity to disrupt linear radio.

By the time you read this, the above specific company examples may not have aged well*, as nothing lasts forever, but the principles remain.

The following are some of the common threads of TAM busting business models:

- A strong core cash-generative business that is a protected source of resilience. Bets on new markets are not made by risking the farm.†
- Long-term growth-oriented leadership that is willing to sacrifice short-term earnings to make multiple, yet carefully evaluated, experimental bets that seed future optionality.
- Flexible/capable independently managed sub-teams, where management have a strong track record of execution.

* An observation we also made when exploring SABMs.

† Unless the farm is under existential threat, then you may have no choice.

Great management is fundamental to the ability to execute a TAM-busting strategy. Identifying TAM busters in advance is hard. Perhaps the best place to start is with management teams that have done it once or twice already, in which case the base rate odds are more favourable that they can do it again.

Conclusion

Owning a diversified basket of independent call options, including the option to attack adjacent and new markets (TAM busting) gets us well along the patient path to prosperity. As investors, we should be looking for firms that are building or buying cheap options. For options to convert to value, you need to survive (resilience) and have the experience to know when and how to capitalise on them.

Having multiple, cheap, long-dated options means we don't need to be geniuses. Options are a powerful form of positioning, and such positioning is far more effective than any attempts at trying to forecast the future. It renders forecasting (which is usually futile anyway) unnecessary.

And time is our friend.

11

Chapter Eleven: Macro for Context, Micro for Conviction

> *For want of a nail the shoe was lost, for want of a shoe the horse was lost, and for want of a horse the rider was lost.*
>
> – Medieval proverb

Macro analysis looks at the bigger picture, the overarching trends and global factors that shape the economic landscape. It's about understanding how geopolitical events, government policies, and global economic trends can influence market movements. On the other hand, micro analysis delves into the specifics, the granular details of individual companies and their potential for growth and profitability. It's about examining financial statements, understanding specific industry trends, and evaluating management quality.

Though a vast amount of time is spent on macro analysis, my sense is that the pursuit of investment returns (at least for an active equity manager) is best served through understanding the micro. This approach is akin to navigating life's broader challenges. One could easily become consumed by the vast and often overwhelming issues that humanity faces–the macro perspective. Yet, it is the personal relationships we cultivate, the interactions we have–the micro perspective–that ultimately define the quality of our lives.

Macro provides the context, but micro provides the conviction.

Very few people have built wealth through a superior knowledge of macroeconomics. It's simply too hard. Imagine if you knew in early 2022 that US interest rates would rise by 5% in just eighteen months. Most market participants armed with that knowledge would have assumed a far worse economy and stock market than the ones we got. And that's with possibly the most important and consequential macro variable of all. There are numerous other examples of situations where perfect foresight of a highly consequential macro variable would have led to the wrong investment conclusion. This fact alone, coupled with the dearth of successful macro investors should be ample evidence not to be distracted by macro prognostications. The stars of macroeconomic forecasts may twinkle enticingly, but they seldom illuminate. Imagine trying to drive a car while looking through the sunroof.

Think of the macro environment as a variable game of "snakes & ladders". At times the board will be infested with snakes. But why worry? An active investor doesn't have to roll the dice. Simply avoiding the snakes is a winning strategy. Holding out for a long ladder is the way to play. In a sense we are exploring an extreme version of the 80/20 principle which explains the tendency for just a few key variables to be responsible for the lion's share of results. For every handful of micro realities that drive actual results, there are likely hundreds of inconsequential contextual macro considerations.

Peter Lynch famously said; "If you spend more than 13 minutes analysing economic and market forecasts, you've wasted 10 minutes." Macro forecasters don't have stubborn facts like NAVs to be troubling themselves with!

Virtually every time I've tried to convert a macro insight into a stock selection, something got lost in translation. Now, whenever I'm asking, 'What's the best way to get exposure to X?', I must remind myself, 'Stop, stop right now' and get back to work.

Conclusion

When it comes to allocating our precious research time, favour the microscope over the telescope.

PART III
CLIFFS & CAR CRASHES

Having found our way onto the patient path our next challenge is to stay on it. All journeys present obstacles and the compounder's journey is no different. As we learned in Part I, the magic of compounding is intrinsically tied to the amount of time spent compounding. Falling off the path is the same as losing time, and from a compounder's perspective time is not just money, it's exponential money. Part III alerts us to the cliffs and the car crashes. Crashes set us back, which is costly, cliffs are fatal. We need to recognise them. Only then can they be avoided.

Unforced investment errors hurt us in multiple ways:

- We take an immediate capital loss.
- Our mental bandwidth is hijacked.
- The capital loss is the equivalent of wasting the original time that was harnessed in earning that capital, now lost.

But that immediate, visible, and quantifiable pain is nothing compared to the unquantifiable and invisible opportunity costs. Firstly, the mental time wasted could have been put to more productive use. Secondly, and more importantly, the lost capital is capital that could have been compounding decades from now. That's the real iceberg. Outsized returns are found on the compounding log curve. Large mistakes knock us back onto a linear curve.* Anything that interrupts compounding has a huge opportunity cost. It's hard to over-emphasise this. You will notice that this section of the book has the most chapters which reflects a deliberate focus on staying clear of the cliffs and car crashes.

* Small mistakes provide useful information. We should learn from them and embrace them. When I said this to my partner she gave me a hug.

12

Chapter Twelve: The Three Stooges

We're not normal people, we're morons.
– Curly Howard

Reducing both the frequency and cost of errors is a key objective of rational capital allocation. Reflecting on my many mistakes, let's look at a few that I have christened *The Three Stooges.* These represent some of the potential car crashes that we want to avoid. Others follow in later chapters.

It's Too Late Larry

While it is often said that the four most dangerous words in investing are "this time is different", perhaps the three most expensive words (in terms of opportunity cost) are "I missed it".* Why is it so psychologically hard for investors to buy more of something that has gone up in price, even if the increase is justified? Personally, I find it much easier to add at falling prices

* And let's not forget the four most important "is time our friend?". Relatedly, I like to suggest that the three most underrated words are "I don't know."

than to buy at increasing prices. There is something in the DNA of a value-oriented investor that does not want to chase things. There also seems to be some psychological regret at play as I berate myself for missing the opportunity to have previously bought at lower prices. Not adding to a great compounder is an error of omission, the opportunity cost of which is large but rarely visible. The same "it's too late" prevarication can cause us to be too slow to sell holdings, especially after large single day falls. To fight this tendency to anchor on past prices it is helpful to remind oneself that in a liquid market every day is a new day that is discounting a new future. The market ignores the psychological path dependency of our prior price points, and so should we.

Cashed-up Curley

As we discussed earlier, cash has its place. But hoarding excess cash is another matter. The question becomes whether the cash holding is a security blanket (a genuine reserve) or a comfort blanket (a crutch)?* Over the

* This is written in the context of an investment manager. Investors will typically have entrusted capital as part of their risk budget and may well expect a manager to be fully invested. For investment managers cash is a drag on returns but in wider personal contexts holding a cash buffer, even beyond the level of comfort blanket, is entirely understandable.

long-term, cash is a poor investment but at times it provides valuable insurance and optionality. There are many factors that influence the amount of cash that one holds. Historically I have held high cash levels and that was a mistake for someone that was managing a modest amount of capital. I think the bar should be higher when managing small amounts of capital as the excuse that there are not enough attractive investment opportunities seems to me an admission that one is not working hard enough or smart enough to find them.

With large amounts of capital (i.e. tens of billions rather than hundreds of millions), the decision to hold cash is more defensible. But even then, it should be recognised that such a decision is a market timing call. Two problems spring to mind. Firstly, market timing is hard. Very few people have demonstrated market timing competence. Secondly, the subsequent market fall needs to be big enough to compensate for the opportunity cost of being invested.*

Moe the Merrier

There are several investors with both excellent long term track records and investment philosophies that I respect. Using their portfolios as a first screen for investment opportunities is an efficient and logical use of time. "Coat-tail investing" is unusual in the degree to which it is easy to copy the greats.

The problem with this "more the merrier" approach is when it substitutes for one's own investment analysis. If an investment has a random price fall, will we have the fortitude to hold or add? And

*The opportunity cost is the return from your invested portfolio.

there are other problems with coat-tailing. The stock acquisition that we have attributed to our famed investor may not have been picked by them at all, but instead by someone else on the team, a new apprentice perhaps. Furthermore, we don't know the portfolio context. The stock may be a hedge for another position rather than an outright high conviction long. Or they may have simply made a mistake. Many people followed Eddie Lampert into Sears, which was understandable given Lampert's investing track record. Retailers have a nasty habit of humbling the greatest investors. Respected investor portfolios are an efficient screen. But the dictum "do your own work" remains.

A related topic for professional investors is the question of team-based decisions or individual decisions. Each has their merits and I've operated in both team-based systems and ones with individual autonomy. Having experienced both approaches my personal preference is for individual autonomy where a sole portfolio manager makes the final decision. The sole portfolio manager can be supported by analysts and challenged by colleagues, but ultimately the decision is owned by one person. Individual biases create ample issues without adding multiplicative behavioural complications that arise from group decisions.

Conclusion

It's never too late to buy a great company or to sell a bad one (tempered by price). Don't hoard excess cash as a crutch. Learn from people we respect but do our own work.

13

Chapter Thirteen: The Frank Filter

It is twice the pleasure to deceive the deceiver.
– Jean de La Fontaine

Groucho Marx observed; "The secret to life is honesty and fair dealing. If you can fake that, you've got it made." Investors are indulged with many ways to lose money. Rationality and due diligence can help protect against the more common errors of paying too much, or underestimating the impact of competitive forces. Losses from overpaying or from competitive weaknesses are painful yet predictable. But what of losses from corporate fraud or dishonesty? Less predictable, equally painful. While for some companies the impact of dishonesty doesn't seem to go much beyond embarrassment, for others it can be franchise threatening or even fatal (WorldCom, Enron, Arthur Andersen). This raises an important question. Can we filter for frankness? In the spirt of avoiding stupidity as an easier endeavour than seeking brilliance, we could begin our exploration with a look at some of the characteristics that may increase the propensity towards dishonesty. These include:

- A history of strong 'adjusted' financial metrics, frequently recast in the most positive light (the next chapter has more to say on this).
- A narcissistic CEO.*
- Companies with flawed incentive schemes (e.g. highly skewed to one metric).
- Companies or industries facing extinction.
- Low return, capital intensive industries, especially prolific borrowers.
- Companies that do business in countries with weak governance.

But the above doesn't answer the harder question. What features would suggest less likelihood of fraud? I asked an engineering friend this question, and he smiled and said, "where people are involved, there is always the risk of fraud." A stark assessment with more than a grain of truth unfortunately.† That said,

* Not to be confused with an obsessive or eccentric CEO. Some of the most effective CEOs are ultra rational but socially awkward.

† Malcolm Gladwell's book, *Talking to Strangers* is a sobering assessment of how we are easily fooled, so read what follows with a smidgen of scepticism.

I suspect investors *may* find refuge at the intersection of character, culture and capital allocation.

1. On Character. Good management leads by example. Results are presented honestly and clearly. Mistakes are admitted early, communicated openly and dealt with promptly. Frequently fanatical, with real skin in the game (high insider ownership where wealth creation is through founder shares or purchased shares held for the long term). Those of good character understand how trust is earned and sustained.

2. On Culture. A good culture reveals itself in a purpose-driven organisation with a strong service ethos. The company is looking to do great work first with a view that profits will then follow. The culture is nurtured with a balanced blend of humility and ambition, rooted in delivering the highest customer surplus.

A high-quality culture is hard to define but you know it when you see it, *feel it* even. It permeates the entire organisation. Employees are all-in on the company mission. Everyone trusts each other to do the right things for customers and for each-other.*

3. On the Craft of Capital Allocation. There is an intellectual honesty that flows from a clearly articulated focus on capital allocation. Returns on capital employed (or in the case of capital light businesses, returns on allocated resources) go to the core of frank performance evaluation. Thoughtful capital alloca-

* In the words of Charlie Munger, they operate in a 'seamless web of deserved trust.'

tors produce transparent financial metrics that can be reconciled to free cash flow and that can be readily understood in the context of the underlying business.

Minnesota as a Metaphor for Trust

We want to avoid untrustworthy companies at all costs. They will take us over the cliff. Trust is like water, life sustaining, yet difficult to grasp. Each of us aspires to be trustworthy, and the world runs smoothly when we can 'reliably rely' on each other. Sadly, trust is elusive. Our trust in corporations, governments and currencies is routinely tested. Something as fundamental as our own memory is fallible. Self-deception is rife.* Deep trust is a scarce and precious resource. Sound investment philosophies are predicated on finding good businesses run by competent and trustworthy management. Such trust is so rare that it is a huge advantage where it does exist. Trustworthy management attracts aligned and motivated teams. These are teams you don't want to have to compete against.

But what is the nature of trust, what does it mean to be trustworthy and how do we calibrate trust? We might categorise trust into two categories, *transactional trust,* and *true trust.*

Think of trust as an elastic. There is a natural bond between most people. The bond can be stretched, but with too much strain it snaps, forever broken (unless tentatively re-tied with an awkward knot). Or consider the cycle of a reservoir. The reservoir is filled with trust sustaining actions, thereby building a trust reserve, but it can be easily depleted through broken promises. The cycle repeats as the trust reservoir is

* Though paradoxically advantageous in an evolutionary context.

slowly filled again, perhaps through genuine apology backed up with enough good behaviour. The elastic and reservoir are helpful concepts, but I think they fail to fully capture the multi-dimensional nature of trust. It is not simply a case of A trusts B, but a more comprehensive A trusts B to do C in circumstance D. We may trust company management not to excessively pay themselves (if for example they are already large shareholders), but that doesn't mean that we can trust them to treat their employees, suppliers, or customers fairly. The elastic and reservoir metaphors feel a little like *transactional trust.*

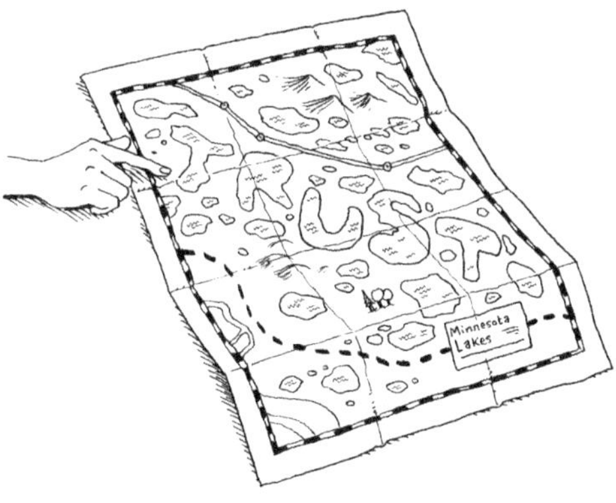

Is there a better metaphor?
This got me thinking about Minnesota with its wonderful water wilderness. Minnesota's multiplicity of lakes nicely reflects the multi-dimensional nature of *true trust.*

The most trustworthy people/companies are constantly filling numerous lakes, sustaining a trusted ecosystem. At the corporate level for example, a long-term oriented leadership team will continually strive to earn and sustain trust with customers, staff, suppliers, regulators, the community, and shareholders. It will fill multiple lakes and will guard against leakage, thereby fostering a true multi-stakeholder win-win environment.

Understanding this wider view of trust may help us in the quest to find genuinely great companies, i.e. those that can durably compound value without dis-enfranchising any part of the ecosystem on which their long-term success relies. Sadly, sustaining trust at scale is often eventually sacrificed in the pursuit of maximum profit. Cory Doctorow has written about how large tech platforms which start out with good intentions, eventually end up abusing trust, a corrosive process he calls *enshittification.** The companies initially signalled trust, but it was transactional and therefore transitory. Be suspicious of transactional trust. Treasure true trust. True trust-based ecosystem sustainers eschew *enshittification.*

Conclusion

The trifecta of character, culture, and thoughtful capital allocation is a good filter for frankness. Deserved trust is rare and powerful. Self-sustaining trust-based ecosystems are even more rare and more valuable. The firm that nurtures and sustains a broad-based trusted ecosystem is a formidable one and deserves to survive and thrive. Be wary of companies that abuse trust or take it for granted. Separate transactional trust from true trust.

* Yves Smith calls it 'crapification'. There is a theme here!

14

Chapter Fourteen: Denominator Dissonance

It is a capital mistake to theorize before one has data. Insensibly one begins to twist facts to suit theories, instead of theories to suit facts.
– Arthur Conan Doyle, Sherlock Holmes

Management teams that have mastered the art of narrative often do so while cherry-picking their numbers in a deliberate distortion of numerical truth. Consider the CFO who boasts of a doubling of market share, but says nothing about the base, i.e. a doubling from what? Doubling share from 2% to 4% in a large competitive market might be very impressive. But what about from 0.0002% to 0.0004% in a small market?

Alternatively, a CEO might crow about a twenty percent increase in sales and say nothing about the prior year level, or an acquisition that enabled the increase, or a sacrifice in margins. Call it "denominator dissonance." When you start looking for it you see it everywhere. Politicians love it. They may talk about crime rates being down. But might that just be reported crime rates because of some administrative quirk in the reporting methodology?

A company celebrates that it added $100 million in sales. That's an absolute number without context. On its own it doesn't mean anything. Or highlighting a large increase in EBITDA while ignoring an increase in borrowings. Selective disclosure writ large.

Then we get commentary of changes in the rates of growth, rather than in absolute levels of growth. For example, stating that a company's rate of growth doubled, is a far cry from a doubling of the absolute base level. A company that grew sales 1% in one year and grew sales 2% in the second year may try to impress with a "doubling of its growth rate". And this is to say nothing of what competitors might have achieved, or tailwinds from inflation or FX movements.

Everything is context dependent and for full context we need to understand both numerators and denominators along with the broader environment of those features for competitors and the industry at large. We are in danger of misinterpreting data in the absence of contextual awareness. Accept nothing at face value.

The elegance of double entry accounting is that every asset has a corresponding liability. This can be spun into two half-truths where one side of the balance sheet is highlighted to the exclusion of the other, while the real truth is in the reconciliation.

When you read a headline that "investors are underweight equities", that's a meaningless statement because, at the system level, all assets are fully allocated always. The question to ask is "which investors are underweight" and "underweight in comparison to what"? Their own history? They will always be underweight against some other category in some other context. It reminds me of the Yogi-ism "that place is so crowded nobody goes there anymore."

Watch the words of management. Are they splitting revenue growth between volume and price and showing the relative contributions of organic growth and growth by acquisition. When they show medium or long-term progress are they cherry picking the starting period? In short, are they demonstrating contextual honesty?

Dissonant Cousins

Denominator dissonance has some close cousins where numbers can be used to deceive us, and we need to be vigilant. These include small sample sizes, mixing up correlation and causation, poorly scaled graphs, lack of replicability, averages versus medians, mistaking statistical significance for practical significance, time distortions and abstractions.*

* Young school children are forced to learn the 'multiplication of fractions', an abstract concept where multiplication is reductive, which doesn't happen in the real world of atoms and things. This confuses both children and teachers, so the exercise frequently gets reframed from 'half multiplied by half' to 'half of a half'. Early education should focus on practical foundations first. The abstract can come later.

Cumulative figures, while seemingly impressive at first glance, can also mislead. Companies might tout cumulative sales or total number of customers acquired without acknowledging the timeframe or the churn rate, an omission that distorts the perception of success.

Seen and Unforeseen

In 1850 French economist Frédéric Bastiat penned an essay highlighting the dangers of overweighing what is visible and near-term at the expense of what is not visible and delayed. Bastiat was distinguishing bad economists who confine their analysis to visible effects from good economists who consider both the effects that can be seen and those effects that must be foreseen. Similarly, the temptation for company management is to highlight near term visible benefits while being silent (and/or ignorant) about future unforeseen consequences, especially if they are incentivised on current results.

Conclusion

Investing is hard enough already without the added burden of trying to figure out whether management is giving us the full story. Be on guard for denominator dissonance and be wary of executives who provide only part of the story, or who are too focussed on disclosing the good without the bad, the gains without the losses, or the picture without the background.

Taken out of context, narratives deceive, and numbers mislead.

15

Chapter Fifteen: On Short Selling – A Shield not a Sword

Do not confuse things that are hard with things that are valuable.

– James Clear

This chapter explores the nature of short selling. In preview, the merits are meagre, and the pitfalls are plentiful. My sense is that short selling appeals to multiple categories of investor:

1. Crusaders/Intellectuals. Some people like to ferret out fraud and hold executives accountable. The best short sellers do society a great service in policing fraud, a service that often requires dogged determination and extreme patience. Grossly overvalued, fraudulent, pointless and/or over leveraged companies that seem destined for failure are intellectually fascinating. Failures are easier to articulate than successes. There is something seductive about spotting a share that is heading to zero, a mental high from being able to foresee the inevitable calamity.

2. Fee Seekers. Having a short capacity in an investment strategy can make it easier to charge performance fees than with a long-only strategy.

3. Risk Managers. Shorts are a useful hedge in specific cases (e.g. pair trades) and can provide investors with a form of insurance on long allocations.

4. Benchmark Investors. There is a category of investors that race in the relative performance derby, benchmark investors. For benchmark investors, short selling is a possible tool to express views relative to a benchmark. Active managers that are managing against a benchmark are always underweight certain constituents and may outright short some constituents to express a high conviction relative view.

5. Opportunity Maximisers. The battle cry of the opportunity maximisers is that the capacity to short improves their investment armoury. In theory a well-executed short portfolio can deliver diversifying profits that can be recycled on the long side, and for the flawless executors that's true. In practice I think it merely adds a faulty weapon. Adding short selling to your investment talents (at least in the pursuit of alpha as distinct from risk management) is primarily an opportunity to shoot yourself in the foot.

Why is short selling so hard?

Short sellers have a valid argument that their space is less crowded, but perhaps there are good reasons for that. The list is long:*

(i) ***Unlimited downside.*** Russian roulette anyone? In practice the downside is probably not unlimited in the same way that the upside on a long holding can't quite be unlimited either. But the downside can absolutely be multiples more than 100% and that's not a great place to be.

(ii) ***Capped upside.*** If you are perfectly right the most you can earn is 100% less funding costs (though you can earn some interest in higher rate environments). There are no 'compounders' in the world of shorting.

(iii) ***Time is your enemy.*** With a maximum return of 100% the longer it takes for your thesis to play out the worse your returns. Even obvious frauds can take many years to crack. In other cases, the reasons for fraud can be complex and well-hidden for longer than you would like. By the time you reach, say, five years your maximum return is 15% per annum (while being continually exposed to the possibility of unlimited loss). Patience doesn't pay.

(iv) ***Swimming against the long-term current.*** Markets go up over time. They have a positive bias. The median long investor gets a satisfactory result, the median short

* What follows pertains to outright shorting as distinct from buying put options.

investor a negative one as they are on the wrong side of the main upward trend, and they also have borrowing costs to factor in. Wealthy short sellers are a rare breed.

(v) ***Psychological negativity.*** Wishing for stock prices to implode is out of sync with a healthy human condition. It's generally better to be a cheerleader than a cynic. Don't get me wrong, all investors need a degree of cynicism, I just wonder whether being exclusively focused on the short side makes for a good personal and professional disposition.

(vi) ***The short squeeze.*** You can get forced out of your trade at an inconvenient time.

The above characteristics make short selling a difficult craft, one that is more suited to defence (risk management/portfolio hedging) than offence (alpha/absolute return generation). In this sense, short selling is possibly fine as a shield (risk management), but not as a sword (absolute alpha).

Might short selling have any place?

In addition to its role as a possible risk management tool, the other area where short sellers may have satisfactory results (in the pursuit of alpha) is in shorting credit (as distinct from equity). A critical and under-appreciated difference between shorting credit and shorting equity is that the risk/reward asymmetry is reversed. When shorting credit your maximum loss is the effective interest cost of the instrument shorted while your possible gain can be multiples of the short cost.

Many readers will be familiar with the movie *The Big Short*. It chronicled how several investors profited from the US housing collapse. What is less well known is that the biggest gains were made shorting credit, not shorting equity. If for example you were short a AAA rated tranche of a securitisation that paid and traded at an effective interest rate of 1% per annum, and, say, it took two years for the securitisation to crack. Your cost was 2%, but if the security ended up only being worth 50 cents on the dollar you would have made 25 times your money. If you shorted the equity in Lehman the most you could have made was 100%. If you shorted its debt, you could have earned many multiples of your investment.

The better pay-off profile in shorting credit still doesn't make it easy but at least the rewards for being right, and the costs of being wrong, are far better compared to shorting equities.

Conclusion

In short, don't bother. When valuations are stretched hold cash instead. If you must short, consider it as a risk management tool, a shield not a sword. And even then, there are arguably better risk management tools.

If you are an alpha hunter, hunt for shorts in the credit world, not the equity world.

16

Chapter Sixteen: Antidotes for Anecdotes

The human mind is a story processor, not a logic processor.

– Jonathan Haidt

"Dad, can you tell me a story." Sound familiar? We can all relate to the power of stories. Those that are told to us, those that we tell ourselves, and those that we tell others. Stories simplify learning, understanding and recall. Stories can motivate us, move us or moor us.

I recently shared a car ride with my friend Stefan. As we drove from Boston to Cape Cod, I was pitching an investment idea. Half-way through explaining why I liked it, Stefan interjected and said, "Lar, just the facts please." This brought a smile to my face, as Stefan and I have often talked about the dangers of coherent stories. Stefan's request was a gentle reminder not to get blinded by the power of story.*

Coherent Stories

We make decisions based on stories, not numbers. Can you remember the last time you decided based on a number? Where no stories exist, we create them. Our brains love to close gaps and package things into neat stories. For most of what we need to do in life, this 'gap-filling' works well as it preserves our precious cognitive load. When it comes to investing however, we can be misled by coherent narratives and once we have them in our heads, we are reluctant to change them (status quo bias). Narrative fallacy and confirmation bias conspire to blind us to where we may be wrong.

> *"All lies in jest, still a man hears what he wants to hear and disregards the rest"*
> *(The Boxer - Simon & Garfunkel).*

We frequently build beliefs based on insufficient evidence, failing to appreciate that the plural of anecdotes is not evidence. "High conviction" concentrated portfolio managers are particularly exposed to

* I appreciate the irony that this paragraph is itself a story (albeit a true one). Seemingly we are all in the entertainment business.

being captured by the power of story, especially if the story/thesis has been true for a long time (a historic compounder). We are sitting comfortably, blind to the impending tornado.

Possible Antidotes

There are two broad approaches to dealing with this problem; prevention & cure ("an ounce of prevention is worth a pound of cure") – what we might call the antidotes to the anecdotes (a.k.a. cures for stories).

Antidote Category A: The Art of Prevention

A.1 - Slow Down. We don't have to be fast; we just need to be right. Our minds tend to get excited about a positive thesis and discount negative data when in such a state. To this end we can force a cooling off period before making an investment. Take a few days or weeks and then re-visit the thesis. Our purportedly compelling idea frequently has warts on it. Better to move on and resume the truffle hunt. For truly great companies, being a few weeks late has negligible opportunity cost.*

To help us slow down, we can use checklists which are rationally and honestly updated (Chapter 19).

A.2 - Cultivate a Scientific Mindset. Evolutionary biologist, Ernst Mayr put it like this: "All interpretations made by a scientist are hypotheses, and all hypotheses are tentative. They must forever be tested, and they must be revised if found to be unsatisfactory. Hence, a change of mind in a scientist, and particular-

* Don't fall into the 'It's too late Larry' trap.

ly a great scientist, is not only not a sign of weakness but rather evidence for continuing attention to the respective problem and an ability to test the hypothesis again and again."

As a discipline, science is robust at filtering out noise. Good scientists (those with 'scientific equipoise') strive to start out with no pre-conceived bias or prejudice. If predictions deduced from any given hypothesis are proven untrue, the hypothesis is rejected. When new information comes to light that is inconsistent with the established thesis, then that thesis must be rejected. Rational investors think like scientists, not defence attorneys.*

A.3 - Check the Distance from the Base Rate. When we make an investment, we are effectively making a prediction. It makes sense to test that prediction against pre-existing realities. For example, if I am investing in a capital-intensive business and I expect double digit free cash-flow margins, I should test that likelihood against what is normal (the base rate) for similar companies. The degree of confidence in my prediction should be inversely proportional to its distance from the base rate, and the variability of comparable businesses from that base rate. It's always sensible to be able to explain what needs to happen for our views to hold water. We don't want to be relying on six impossible things before breakfast.

* Renaissance Technologies, probably the most successful hedge fund of all time, only hired scientists. As articulated by the late founder Jim Simons: "We don't hire people from business schools. We don't hire people from Wall Street. We hire people who have done good science."

A.4 - Brain splits. Edward de Bono has done a lot of practical work on how our brains work. His 'Six Thinking Hats' framework forces us to differentiate between facts, opinions and feelings. For example, if a group of people are analysing an investment opportunity, the thinking hats approach would parse the discussion into distinct phases. The Black Hat phase covers risks, weaknesses & dangers. During that part of the discussion, everyone "wears" the Black Hat. Only when all the risks have been discussed does the group switch hats to another colour, for example to the Red Hat which deals with feelings. (White Hat covers facts, Blue Hat covers process, Yellow Hat covers benefits, and the Green Hat covers creativity). This process of splitting the brain into parallel thinking by forcing everyone to work on the same track at the same time is very effective at making and understanding decisions.

I used to work for a gifted tax consultant and mentor* who opened all his written advice with a paragraph titled "Facts as understood." Only from there did he move on to giving an opinion.

A.5 - Different Roles. The classic analyst/portfolio manager distinction is helpful here as is having a devil's advocate. Better still is to hear, and be able to understand, the view of someone who:

- genuinely holds an opposing view (as it is too convenient to discount the 'devil's advocate' view).
- is someone we respect.
- has a different background from us.
- is willing to challenge us.

* Ian Young

A.6 - Pre-Mortems. Credited to Gary Klein, a pre-mortem is the act of writing down what has gone wrong in advance of such a possibility. Assume that your prospective investment has failed miserably and write the news release of what went wrong. Better still, ask a few people to independently write a pre-mortem. This is not an exercise in outlining what might go wrong but an articulation of what did go wrong. The subtle shift engages a different part of our brain to uncover a wider appreciation of the number of ways in which things can and do go wrong. The pre-mortem however can only stretch our imagination, it won't help us with the "unknown unknowns" and we need to be alive to the first signs of those.

A.7 - Be Careful who you Listen to. Because stories are so powerful, we need to be careful about the stories we allow ourselves to hear. Avoid untrustworthy or unreliable storytellers or sources. To paraphrase Shakespeare, we don't need to be listening to tales told by an idiot, full of sound and fury, signifying nothing. Prioritise listening to those with real skin in the game and proven results. Everyone else is less credible.

A.8 - Contrary Articulation Bar. Don't allow yourself to conclude on a matter until you can perfectly articulate the contrary view. As F. Scott Fitzgerald astutely pointed out; "The test of a first-rate intelligence is the ability to hold two opposed ideas in mind at the same time and still retain the ability to function." Law students prepare for moot court without knowing which side they are arguing. We learn a lot when we truly seek to understand the other side.

Antidote Category B: Remedial Actions

*B.1 - "Find Joy in Changing your Mind".** Changing our minds is cognitively expensive and socially distasteful. To be able to find joy in changing our mind is unconventional, yet powerful. If we can cultivate our personal philosophy as one where we genuinely find joy in changing our minds, we are in a sense using the power of story to hack the power of story.

This is the approach taken by Charles Darwin who truly got excited when he found any evidence that disagreed with his previously held views. On stumbling upon such evidence, he would immediately write it down to give it more salience. Thoughtful investors demonstrate epistemic rationality, the practice of forming beliefs that accurately reflect the real world as closely as possible. This philosophy can be embedded over time through the practice of changing our minds more often and being open with others on why we genuinely find joy in doing so. We can build our own narratives as to why this is the case (for example it's always nice to be a little less naive today than we were yesterday).

A practical approach here is to make the default assumption that, say, 20%, of what we believe on any topic/thesis is simply wrong and our ongoing quest is to find out which 20% and why.

B.2 - Consider the Opportunity Cost. It is helpful to recognise that all decisions have opportunity costs. Not changing our minds can carry the opportunity cost of missing out on a better solution. Good is the enemy of great.

* Thanks to Patrick McNulty for the inspiration for this motto.

B.3 - Clear the Decks. To counter the endowment effect, confirmation, and status quo biases, we could occasionally sell our entire portfolio (or have it randomly forced upon us like forced annual leave). I don't mean this as an intellectual exercise of approaching our portfolio with fresh eyes *as if* we didn't own it; I suggest we make the physical sale and start afresh. If we are worried about being out of the market while reconsidering our re-investment portfolio allocation, we can temporarily invest the proceeds in an index fund pending reallocation. The clarity brought about by an actual sale is real. For starters the endowment effect is gone. Our brains now shift into a brand-new starting frame of reference. On the few occasions where I have seen colleagues forced to temporarily liquidate a portfolio, they have never bought back the same holdings that they held before the forced sale.

Given the transaction costs, this is probably something that should only be practiced infrequently, perhaps once every few years. (Furthermore, an external investor may see this as an expensive approach to mental discipline. Many of the approaches that people are comfortable taking with their own money are harder to defend when managing external capital, even when such approaches make financial sense).

In his book *No Bull*, Michael Steinhardt spoke about his occasional decision to close out all his positions when he felt the portfolio was not in sync with the market and that he would be better off with a clean slate. "In an instant, I would have a clean position sheet. Sometimes it felt refreshing to start over, all in cash, and to build a portfolio of names that represented our strongest positions and cut us free from wishy-washy holdings."

B.4 - Automatic Stop-losses. If we can't overcome a bias (e.g. holding onto losers through loss aversion or endowment effects), stop losses are one way to deal with the consequences of our bias. We take the decision away from our messy brains and can always re-group later and re-instate the purchase.* Automatic stop losses are simply a version of quant and rule-based strategies that are designed to keep some of the emotion out of investing. Traders use stop losses, technical rules, or other overlays to protect their total capital base, caring less about changing individual positions and more about the overall result (it is fine to lose 60% of the time if the quantum of gains from the 40% winning trades delivers a disproportionate gain).

B.5 - Say Less. While we need to be able to articulate our thesis to test our reasoning with knowledgeable sceptics, we should avoid becoming an evangelist for any investment. Public declarations are harder to pull back from especially if you have had to defend a view in public. Blinkers go on (and stay on) when in defence mode. When we are lecturing, we can't be learning.

* A variant I try to practice is that if any of my stocks falls by 20% or more, I either add to the position or exit it entirely. It's the poker equivalent of 'raise or fold', but don't 'stick' as that too closely resembles a rabbit caught in the headlights.

Conclusion

There is a saying that we should never let the facts get in the way of a good story. When it comes to investing, we should never let a good story get in the way of the facts.

The discipline of investing requires a careful sifting of narrative and data. It's crucial to cultivate a mindset that prioritises facts and seeks to challenge and test our own narratives rigorously. By combining scientific scepticism with practical reflection, we can protect ourselves from the seductive pull of compelling stories.*

* This is from the perspective of an investor making an investment decision (weighing factors with the right amount of contextual credit). For company leadership teams, narrative is hugely important in vision building, attracting staff, sales, and finding investors (I see the irony). It's precisely because narrative is so powerful that investors need an antidote.

17

Chapter Seventeen: Leverage & the Lazy Man's Load

> *Once you view debt as narrowing what you can endure in a volatile world, you see it as a constraint on the asset that matters most: having options and flexibility.*
>
> – Morgan Housel

When I was a young boy, my dad encouraged me to help with the manual labour around the garden of our house. Occasionally he would stop me as I pushed an overloaded wheelbarrow and point out that I was carrying a "lazy man's load." It took a toppling over of the wheelbarrow a few times for me to fully appreciate the lesson. Leverage is a lot like an over-loaded wheelbarrow; increased short term productivity at the risk of ruin. Leverage magnifies results. Leverage can't make a bad investment good, but it can force an inopportune exit from an otherwise good investment, a subtly unsatisfactory asymmetry.

There are three obvious categories of leverage that sensible investors will want to understand before allocating capital. The first category is financial leverage or borrowing and we need to be sensitive to the amount, the terms and the availability. The second is operating leverage, the most common component of which is the level of fixed costs in a business. The third category is off balance sheet leverage (e.g. leases, pensions, derivatives, warranties, JV commitments). Most of the time the sources of leverage are obvious, but there are situations when even the most diligent investors get blind-sided.

Examples of some of the less obvious sources of leverage are:

- *Leveraged Customers or Leveraged Industry Structure.* If your customers are highly leveraged, this makes them vulnerable, and by association you are vulnerable.
- *Single or Concentrated Leverage Provider.* The US for-profit education sector relies on Government guarantees to help students borrow for tuition fees. Certain equipment exporters rely on one or more state-subsidised credit insurers. Absent a satisfactory alternate source of funding, everyone in the sector is vulnerable to changes in the credit policies of the existing providers.
- *Working Capital Terms.* If an industry suffers a shock through the default of one player, it can drive some or all the other participants to tighten credit terms thereby squeezing working capital.
- *Others.* Cartel structures, regulatory reliefs, subsidies, long-term contracts (especially if index linked), large supplier or customer concentrations.

Advantageous Divergence – Finding Strength in Liabilities

While numerous fortunes have been built through leverage, especially in property, more fortunes have been lost through leverage than in any other way. It is the surest way to be taken off the patient path, a car crash waiting to happen. Warren Buffett famously said of leverage, that if you're smart you don't need it, but if you're not smart, you've no business using it. What's more interesting, is that he built his fortune on leverage, but, critically, it was leverage of the friendly variety, which brings us to a wider discussion of the value and nature of *Friendly Financial Leverage.*

Let's investigate four different sources of friendly financial leverage.

Source One: Insurance Float

Insurance companies collect cash through insurance premia. That cash is received upfront, ahead of any event-based insurance claims. In a well-managed, profitable, diversified insurance business, that cash can be invested. For a profitable insurer this float (premia received) costs nothing to service, so it is like interest free debt, and, for a growing business, it has no fixed maturity date. Interest-free debt that you don't have to repay, now that's friendly! The float is invested predominantly in fixed income securities, and the returns accrue to the insurance company.

Berkshire Hathaway, Markel Corporation, and Fairfax Financial all benefit from float as they run growing profitable insurance businesses and invest a component of their float in income generating fixed income assets, and, to a lesser degree given regulatory capital constraints, equity securities. Their success in accessing this friendly source of leverage has not gone unnoticed and many investment managers have sought (mostly unsuccessfully) to emulate the model. Running a profitable insurance business is harder than it looks, so this source of leverage is only available to those with the competence to run a profitable business in what is a commoditised industry. Those attracted to the sector by the benefits of float had better be disciplined insurance operators, otherwise they are tourists in hostile territory.

The value of float is lower in low interest rate environments, like the one that we had up until 2022. As rates have risen recently the value of float is also rising, at least for those insurers that were good at risk managing their fixed income portfolios. Those that kept duration short in the low interest rate environment have been able to re-invest into higher income securities through 2023 and into 2024. The combination of friendly financial leverage and investment acumen led to valuable optionality.

Source Two: Asset Management

As we learned in Part II, the business model of many asset managers (e.g., KKR, Intermediate Capital Group and Brookfield Corporation) is to invest their own balance sheet capital alongside money that they manage on behalf of external investors. The external investor capital is affectionately known in the industry as OPM*, i.e. *Other People's Money,* and it is one of the friendliest sources of financial leverage there is.

For example, let's assume that Brookfield invests $20 of its own balance sheet capital alongside $80 from its co-investors and then purchases a $100 asset. Say the asset appreciates 10% and is then sold one year later, what is Brookfield's return? 10% gain on its $20 investment is $2 but it also collects a fee on the managed capital, say 2% (including performance fees). That's 2% of the $80 or $1.60. $2.00 + $1.60 = $3.60 on initial equity of $20 which is a healthy 18% return on capital. Turning a 10% return into an 18% return, with virtually no additional risk, is highly advantaged compared to the person investing without the benefit of OPM.

Source Three: Negative Working Capital

Businesses with negative working capital receive their sales proceeds before they have to pay their suppliers. They are paid cash upfront by their customers. Examples include many retailers (including online and discount retailers), restaurants, and telecommunications companies. Multilevel marketing businesses are also very cash-generative during their growth phase. These businesses can use negative working capital to

* Not quite 'opium', but nearly as addictive.

fund growth (instead of issuing dilutive equity capital). UK businesses like Applegreen (convenience stores) and DFS Furniture (sofas) have historically been able to fund growth through an ever-increasing accounts payable balance. So have Amazon, Aldi, and Lidl.

As with insurance float, this source of friendly leverage is only useful when a business is at least steady, or preferably growing. Problems emerge if the business shrinks, in which case the leverage effectively becomes due. This happened to many enterprises during 2020 when the pandemic forced business shutdowns. Given this risk of reversal, negative working capital, while powerful, is not the friendliest source of advantage and those companies that benefit from it, are well advised not to rely on it.

Source Four: Deferred Tax

Deferred tax is akin to an interest free loan. Good tax planning can facilitate deferrals for long periods. A common example is capital gains tax (CGT), which only becomes due on the sale of an asset. Assume you own an asset that cost $100 and is now worth $500 and that the CGT rate is 30%. A sale of the asset would trigger a cash tax cost of $120 leaving only $380 ($500 less $120 tax) to re-invest. Rather than pay the tax and only have $380 to re-invest, many prefer to hold the asset and let the $500 continue working (the economic equivalent of a $500 asset part-funded by an interest free loan of $120).

Knowing that an asset held for the long-term can benefit from deferred tax can have the added benefit of forcing one to be more diligent at the outset in their choice of asset. Put differently, deferred tax is a valuable source of leverage for the right asset, namely an asset that has a long growth runway. We are inclined to think more carefully about the purchase of an investment that we intend to hold for a decade or more.

While the tax bill eventually comes due, there are occasions where it might not. For example, my tax mentor used to say, "death cures CGT". In many jurisdictions, assets can pass on to an estate without triggering a CGT liability.* In certain other circumstances tax exempt asset swaps are available, again extending the deferral period.

The ability to defer, reduce or eliminate tax is a large driver of returns in the private equity industry. The tax deductibility of interest facilitates building wealth. Deferred tax was a substantial component of how John Malone built Liberty Global, and countless others (e.g., railroads through accelerated depreciation and real estate operators) have benefited from deferred tax as a source of friendly financial leverage.

Other Sources

Originally, I considered including some specific forms of debt like:

- Perpetual, or long-dated, callable, low-cost, fixed-rate fixed debt.
- Non-recourse debt (e.g., securitisations).

While these are arguably friendly types of leverage, it's hard to find examples of companies uniquely exploiting such sources to derive a sustainable structural advantage.

Perhaps sovereigns can? Given investors occasional willingness to accept negative real yields, why would

* We still need to consider inheritance or other estate taxes.

a sovereign not issue low-cost fixed rate perpetual, or 100-year, sovereign bonds and invest the proceeds in productive assets? Imagine Germany borrowing, say, €500 billion in 100-year fixed rate bonds and investing the proceeds in the S&P 500! Relatedly, Stan Druckenmiller recently criticised Janet Yellen, for what he described as "the biggest blunder in Treasury history" for not issuing US long-term treasuries when rates were insanely low.

Friendly Financial Leverage for Individuals

I've always felt that long-term debt to purchase the home that one lives in, is leverage of the friendly variety, provided you don't overpay for the house, and you can handle the debt service costs. The benefits are clear:

- An amortising loan is a way of forced saving.
- You get to live in (i.e., "consume") the asset.
- It is a hedge against inflation as the loan is repaid in nominal dollars while your home is likely to appreciate with inflation.* In fact, if you are worried about inflation, locking in low-rate, long-term, fixed-rate debt is a great hedge. In the US, individuals can refinance fixed-rate debt without penalty, which is a valuable free option if a better financing option emerges.
- Gains on the sale of a family home are often tax free.

* Though we should be careful not to exclude ongoing repairs which are a partial offset.

Conclusion

Leverage can be lovely or lethal depending on its nature and its use. Most of the time it's best avoided as it increases the risk of being knocked off the patient path. It's a cliff best avoided. However, for a small cohort of businesses there is a category of friendly financial leverage that allows them to have their cake and eat it too.

18

Chapter Eighteen: Commodity Investing

Every sin is the result of a collaboration.

– Seneca.

Commodity investing can be rewarding, but for the most part it isn't. The most common definition of a commodity business is one which has no control over the sales price of its product. It is a price taker rather than a price giver. The obvious example, and the subject of this chapter, is resource companies, but lots of other businesses have no control over their average selling price. If one invests in a commodity company, and holds that investment for a long time, the gravity of poor industry returns virtually assures a poor result. It doesn't matter how useful the underlying commodity is. Think of the value of a barrel of oil in terms of man hours worked, which by some estimates is over 20,000 hours. At $100 per barrel that's $0.005 per hour, which is almost free. There is an enormous disconnect between price and value, and the commodity seller can't capture a share of that value. Or consider a can of Coca-Cola. How much value goes to the can manufacturer, or the aluminium supplier? Not much.

There are exceptions of course, but on average, commodity investing is fraught with issues. Numerous diligent and smart investors have learned this the hard way. I remember a phenomenal write-up of Chesapeake in *Outstanding Investor Digest.** It was an articulate and brilliantly argued investment thesis, one of the best I'd read. It was widely shared. It was widely followed. It was an investment nightmare. Some years later when I worked at KKR a colleague did amazing work on Fred Olsen. The quality of his analysis was so good that I was embarrassed by my own work. The thesis made a ton of sense with asymmetric upside and minimal downside. The downside prevailed. I was not immune from trying. My choice of peculiar poison was the debt on oil rigs. I built a physical library of files that almost needed an extension to my office. Results were not terrible, but they

* Sadly, no longer in print.

came with a high opportunity cost. One day my mind flipped, and I duly accompanied my horde of rig files to the shredder, like a smoker ripping up his cigarette packs and quitting for good.*

What follows is a brief exploration of the challenges of commodity investing.

The Seven Challenges of Commodity Investing

Challenge #1: Anchor of Poor Industry Returns.
Commodity industries are low return industries that act as an anchor/drag on returns for most industry participants. Significant capabilities, effort or luck are required to avoid the industry dynamics for any sustained period.†

Challenge #2: Low Returns attract Leverage.
Because industry returns on capital employed are mediocre, commodity companies often add leverage to get to a return on equity threshold that is sufficient to attract equity capital. Combining leverage and commodity businesses is an explosive mix that leads to boom-and-bust cycles. Fortunes can be made on the upswings that are quickly given back when the cycle turns. A commodity business is risky, and leverage exacerbates the situation.

Challenge #3: Confusing Return of Capital for Return on Capital.
When many investors look at valuation multiples like price earnings ratios for mining or exploration companies, they fail to appropriately adjust for the fact that

* I wish it was for good. A recent relapse cost me 1% of NAV.

† Some explorers suffer the additional capital burden of having to pre-reserve decommissioning costs.

the companies have limited life assets. As minerals are extracted from the ground, the company's assets are shrinking. Using Ben Grahams apt analogy about the market being a voting machine in the short term, and a weighing machine in the long run, resource companies are rapidly losing weight, unless they are spending considerable capex on weight supplements.

Challenge #4: Compensating for Congenital Optimism.

A colleague of mine once said that the best commodity company CEOs were "optimists with stamina." Having met dozens of resource patch CEOs I can relate to his sentiment. The industry seems to attract enthusiastic optimists with a zealous belief in their prospects. Stan Druckenmiller reportedly made the following wry remark at a Florida dinner in 2015: "I don't mean to offend any Texans in the room, but if you ever met anybody from Texas, those guys know how to gamble, and if you let them stick a hole in the ground with your money, they're going to do it."

Challenge #5: Disproportionate re-investment Risk.

Resource companies are continually re-investing to replenish their resources so the value of the company you are buying is based primarily on the long-run capital allocation skills of management. The quality of those skills is difficult to judge in an industry that is not conducive to re-investing at high returns.

Challenge #6: Market Timing.

Very few people can call commodity cycles, yet to make outsized returns almost by definition requires superior market timing decisions for both the purchase and exit of investments.

Challenge #7: Valuation Error.

The job of an investor is to value companies and buy their shares when they trade at a sufficient discount to assessed fair value. The valuation exercise for commodity companies is difficult with a high margin of error. In practice a probability-based valuation approach is warranted and there will be a wider than normal distribution of possible valuation outcomes. There are further challenges, some jurisdictional (rule of law, corruption) others geological (you never really know what you have until you have finished digging or drilling) which conspire to make commodity investing hard. It reminds me of a humorous Australian book by Trevor Sykes, *Blue Sky Mines.* The common theme was to promote the great prospect but to never drill a hole! Here is an extract from the back cover.

Warning:
This Company is Deeply
Speculative Indeed

Welcome to the world of Blue Sky Mines (No Liability Except At Gunpoint), The worst run company in Australia.

The chairman is Sir Mark Time, an old drone who has never realised what crimes are being committed at his board meetings. His larcenous board comprises Pierpont the columnist, Bottle the geologist, Spender the accountant and Penwiper the poor but dishonest company secretary.

Their prime property is the Last Card scheelite mine. That is, it is a scheelite mine whenever it suits the board. If gold or nickel is more fashionable, Last Card is a gold or nickel mine. The board, you see, believes in flexibility.

Given the above backdrop many sensible investors ignore commodity companies entirely, and, understandably, put commodity investing in the 'too hard' basket, calling a speculative spade a speculative spade.

If your preference is to retain a flexible mandate, the difficulty of making money in commodity investing should at least put this category in the 'high bar' basket. Here we might insist on:

- unlevered low-cost producers
- with long-life high-quality reserves
- in stable jurisdictions
- with capital friendly private property rights
- run by honest management teams that understand capital allocation.

On this last point, there is a recent crop of commodity companies that, having been ignored by the market, and finding it difficult to secure approvals for expansion projects, have switched to stock-buy backs and dividends, leading to outsized shareholder returns.

Royalty Companies

Despite the challenges faced by traditional commodity companies, there is a lesser-known category of royalty companies, which operate under a markedly different and more favourable model. These companies hold sub-surface mineral rights, allowing them to earn a percentage of the revenue from the extraction of natural resources. This model is predominantly found in the United States, rooted in the nature of "fee-simple" land ownership, which permits the private ownership of mineral rights below the surface.

Importantly, royalty companies do not engage in any direct operations; they are solely asset owners. This results in exceptionally high operating margins since they benefit from the rising prices of commodities via their revenue percentage without bearing the costs associated with extraction. Additionally, they gain from advancements in technology that enhance resource extraction efficiency.

While most mineral royalties are privately owned there is a growing category of US investible public royalty companies across energy, precious metals, and base metals.

Conclusion

Most commodity companies are car crashes on the patient path, best avoided. Cyclicality, low returns, and leverage constitute a motley mix. If you want exposure to commodities, spend time studying royalty companies.

19

Chapter Nineteen: Evolving Checklists

If you don't have time to do it right, when will you have time to do it over?

– John Wooden

A good investment checklist helps us avoid the cliffs and car crashes. It's a navigation tool that should evolve with changes in the investment terrain. I've experimented with longer ones and shorter ones. The current iteration as of 2024 is below. Each category is rated a green (yes), amber (reasonable) or red (no) and includes a rationale for the characterisation.

Checklists can't do the work for us. They can however illuminate blind spots and help us focus on the most important risk and value drivers. I've never found an investment that was green on all categories, but the exercise of visually ranking each holding, calibrates relative risks and opportunities.

Investment Checklist / Quality Criteria
Structurally Advantaged Business Model
Stable/Supportive Country Exposure
Organic Sales Growth
Margin Expansion
"Non-linear" Growth Potential
Management Competence, Alignment & Integrity
Meaningful Insider Ownership
Shareholder Alignment
Quality & Competitive Positioning Improving
Clear Accounting/Cash Conversion
High Existing and Re-investment ROIC
Low Leverage (including pension and OBS liabilities)
Low Capital Intensity
Low Concentration, Capital Markets or other "Cliff" Risks
Robust Against Structural/Technological Challenges
Compelling Valuation

Structurally Advantaged Business Model. We explored SABMs in Chapter 5. Very few companies are structurally advantaged and even fewer can be found at a compelling valuation. For advantaged companies, a reasonable price will do just fine.

Stable/Supportive Country Exposure. The highest long-term equity returns from various stock markets correlate strongly with a stable and capital friendly rule of law (e.g. US*, Canada, Australia, UK, and Scandinavia). The returns for going off-piste need to be attractive and position sizes moderate, as recent inves-

* Operating in a country like the US is still not a guarantee for every sector. Politics and regulatory regimes change. 2023 was the first year in a long time that I'd seen Buffet, the US's biggest cheerleader, bemoan whether profits in Berkshire's utility businesses would be regulated away.

tors in Russian equities have learned. Tortoises are inclined to invest only in stable jurisdictions, unwilling to risk a zero in the compounding exponent.

Organic Sales Growth. Organic growth is oxygen, and most healthy companies demonstrate reasonable and predictable organic growth. Good talent is attracted to growing companies and profitable growth underpins the financial capacity to sow the seeds of future growth. Some of my biggest losses have come from low/no growth companies bought at optically cheap prices.

Margin Expansion. The absence of margin expansion is not always a problem. For example, scale economics shared businesses sensibly keep margins flat in pursuit of absolute market share. More broadly, knowing where we are in the margin cycle is a critical value driver. An under-earning business bought at a low multiple can deliver wonderful returns.

"Non-linear" Growth Potential. For the "right tail" chasers that we met in Chapter 4, this is a critical element. Some businesses are constrained by physics or size and can't scale exponentially without also scaling capital employed. Real estate and heavy machinery manufacturing are examples. Other businesses like software or capital-light financial services can grow at rates disproportionate to capital employed.

For public companies, the businesses themselves don't necessarily need to exponentially scale to facilitate non-linear investment outcomes. If management teams exploit the opportunity to buy back a lot of stock cheaply, shareholders can get non-linear results.

Non-linearity (high-upside, low-downside) is an insanely powerful positive asymmetry. Having exposure to positive non-linearity means we don't need to be right as often, because when we are right it can cover a multitude of poor decisions elsewhere.

This concept applies to all aspects of life. Most of the great things in my life have come down to just a handful of non-linear situations, whether that's in terms of who I married, the friends I've made, people who mentored me, or those friends who entrusted me with their capital.

Non-linearity is joined at the hip with optionality. We return to the power of resilience plus optionality. Build options and survive long enough to exercise them. When you have options, time is your friend. Their value increases with time.*

Management Competence, Alignment & Integrity. The trifecta of competence, integrity, and alignment is exceptionally rare. Warren Buffet is the luminary here, working for a modest salary and earning his keep entirely side-by-side with shareholders. Founder-led businesses with a substantial share ownership tend to be well aligned.

By contrast, most public companies are rife with agency issues. Of all the things I've learned from visceral experience this is the most compelling. The gulf between 'management for rent' and shareholder aligned management is night and day. It's not even an apples to oranges comparison. It's a difference in kind.

* If you wish to dig deeper Nassim Taleb's *Antifragile* is a great place to start.

This difference may not be obvious at first, but it's one that time reveals as critical.

Meaningful Insider Ownership. Again, this is about reducing agency issues.

Quality & Competitive Positioning Improving. The best companies never stop widening their competitive advantage. This requires a customer-oriented mindset. Too often when companies get themselves into a strong position, they start abusing one or more of their stakeholders.*

Clear Accounting/Cash Conversion. A focus on cash avoids complexity and "jam-tomorrow" traps. It reduces the likelihood of being taken in by frauds or thieves. I *deeply* respect businesses that are honest and clear in their accounting (handily passing the *Frank Filter* that we met in Chapter 13).

High Existing and Re-investment ROIC. Return on Invested Capital is the fundamental value driver over any reasonable investment horizon. "*ROE is DestinE*". The best compounders have the runway to continue investing at high returns. Remember our *High ROIC Cookie Cutters* from Chapter 5.

Low Leverage (Including pension and off-balance-sheet liabilities). Unless we are dealing with "friendly financial leverage", then high leverage of any form is generally either best avoided, or our investment posi-

* This reminds me of the observation that money doesn't change people, it reveals them.

tions need to be sized as option positions. Overly levered entities take the torturous path from leveraged to languishing and ultimately lamentable.

Low Capital Intensity. All else equal, higher capital requirements tend to lower investor returns. That said, occasionally, high capital requirements in rational oligopolistic markets can act as a barrier to entry enabling the oligopolistic structure to endure and to support high returns.

Low Concentration, Capital Markets, or other "Cliff" Risks. Risk concentrations are another form of unfriendly leverage, best avoided.

Robust against Structural/Technological Challenges. This risk is increasingly relevant as technology and business models advance. There is a saying that "in the end everything is a toaster", i.e. everything is commoditised eventually as the nature of capitalism virtually ensures. You could go further and say, "in the end everything is toast", which over a sufficiently long-time frame is true of most things. The purpose of having this on our checklist is to keep alive to the continued possibility that our investment will suffer the fate of Yellow Pages directories, Kodak cameras or Blackberry phones.

Compelling Valuation. Of all the variables that have driven my historical returns, starting valuation has been the most consequential.
Cost is crucial. This bears repeating. Cost is crucial. Instead of framing valuation in terms of "what's it

worth", I prefer to ask what's the forward expected return over the next three to five years based on reasonable assumptions. And then break down the sources of those forward expected returns between dividend yield, earnings reinvestment returns, organic growth and change in valuation multiple (multiple expansion is attributed the least, if any value, but risk of multiple contraction is fully accounted for).

Relative Weightings in the Checklist. I've not weighted the checklist as to do so would result in misleading false precision. A combination of a reasonable valuation, a structurally advantaged business model and solid organic growth has tended to work out very well. Problem areas have come from underappreciating leverage, concentrations (both obvious and hidden), and misaligned management.

In addition to the above checklist items, for each investment I also identify the few key value drivers which are then assessed as to their likely outlook, and, just as critically, their degree of predictability.

Key Value Drivers	Outlook	Predictability
Value Driver 1		
Value Driver 2		
Value Driver 3		

Ideally, the outlook for the main value drivers will be supportive, and with a high degree of predictability. If nothing else, the exercise forces some intellectual honesty. I may have a strong view on the outlook for something, but what is the base rate of predictability of such a forecast?

Position Sizing. Related to our discussion of diversification and concentration, position sizing is a key practical consideration, at both the individual stock level and in the context of the economic correlation between holdings. Position sizing is arguably more important than win rate (i.e., the percentage of profitable to unprofitable investments). Effective position sizing is about how much you earn when you are right and how little you lose when you are wrong. Over my investment career I've only twice had position sizes of 15% or more (at cost), and both were within my circle of competence.*

Postmortem. Once we have exited a holding it is good practice to review the outcome of both our winners and our losers. To make this a little more real I had the following stamp manufactured which forces me to distinguish between process and outcome, and between luck and skill.

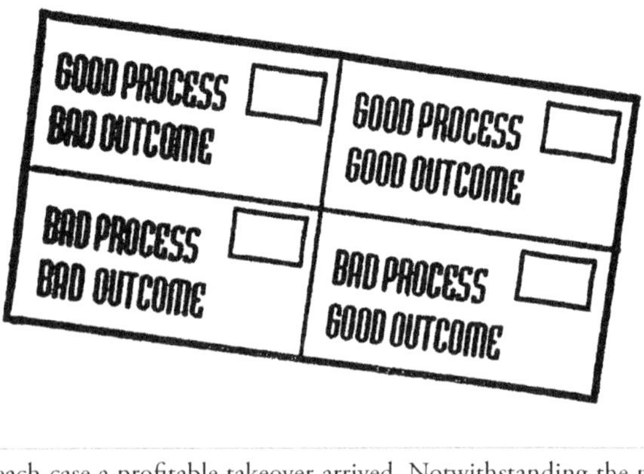

* In each case a profitable takeover arrived. Notwithstanding the more than satisfactory outcome, I still think taking 15% positions was perhaps a little too risky or arrogant or both. I'd never have the chutzpah that Soros showed when he had Druckenmiller upsize his short Sterling bet.

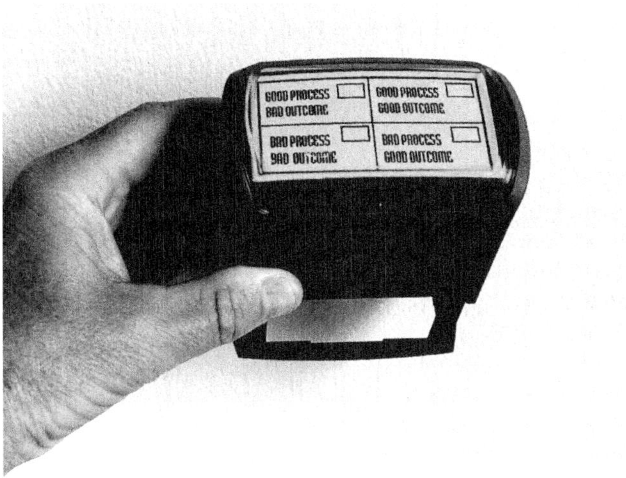

Conclusion

Checklists exist to steer us clear of the cliffs and to avoid the car crashes. Not having one is like flying blind. They reveal both what hurts us and what helps us. They hold us accountable and keep us rational. A checklist in the hand is worth two in the mind.

PART IV
LESSONS FROM THE ROAD

Welcome to the final strait. Here you will find topics of personal interest borne from the visceral experience of over three decades navigating the road, the first twenty years investing my own capital, and the most recent decade as a fiduciary.

I'm still relatively new to the craft* so this is the shortest part of the book, but it was the most fun to write. With some luck, hopefully I'll be doing this for a few more decades, in which case I can revisit everything, and blush at how little I knew in 2024.

* As you may have already noticed ☺.

20

Chapter Twenty: The Vicarious Visceral Gap

The fool doth think he is wise, but the wise man knows himself to be a fool.
- William Shakespeare, As You Like It

In my twenties, I worked for a merchant bank in Sydney, Australia. My office was near the Australian Stock Exchange, and I would go there during my lunch break to watch stock tickers float by on a large screen that was visible from the street. Australia has a very active stock market including numerous resource companies. My office colleagues were regular mining stock investors, which in retrospect was more entertainment than investing. At the same time, the Australian government was in an active program of privatising state companies through Initial Public Offerings ('IPOs'), and those IPOs were nearly always priced attractively to ensure "success". Securing an allocation seemed like, and largely was, a surefire way to earn a quick day-one profit. You could take the proceeds and go again with the next one. For those of us with limited personal capital, this almost looked like free money. We thought we were legends. I'd later learn that mining companies and IPOs are mostly* best avoided, but that's where my initial interest was born.

Making money in the stock market is intoxicating as it doesn't look like real work. Many people, once they get a taste of the game, very quickly decide that they want to learn everything they can about it. I was no different and must have read, to the exclusion of mostly everything else, hundreds of investment books in those early years. A good book represents amazing value for money. For less than the cost of a nice meal out, and a few hours of reading time, we can access the wisdom of what may have amounted to years of work by the author. This vicarious learning is a super way to broaden and deepen our understanding. While reading is wonderful, it is no substitute for actually doing something as the medical world knows only too well with its "see one, do one, teach one" philosophy.

Because I read a lot about investing, I thought I knew a lot, but as soon as I was managing capital for others it became clear how little I knew.† There is a vast chasm between vicarious and visceral learning. It is only with the passing years that one recognises how vast the chasm is. Knowing something intellectually and implementing something practically are simply not the same. They are not even close. I'm embarrassed as to how much wider that gap is than I thought it would be. It's almost as if you must put your hand on

* I say "mostly" here. Everything has a price and the context matters. You will find very few, if any, absolutes throughout this book, because circumstances constantly change.

† I was like the old man who fell into a well because I couldn't see that well.

that hot stove to know that you shouldn't. Reading about hot stoves is insufficient. The visceral mistake is seared in one's brain in a way that the vicarious one never is.*

I had read plenty about the perils of leverage, weak management, poor incentives, illiquidity, commodity businesses, complexity, 'adjusted' earnings, and over-concentration. And I still managed to find myself in multiple real-world situations where one or more of those perils gave me my head in a handbasket. And if that was just my own money, it may be ok, but when you are a fiduciary of other people's capital it's another story altogether. That hot stove leaves a blister and a permanent scar.

If you are entrusting your capital to an investment manager, all else equal, it makes sense to choose a seasoned one.† If, by contrast, you are starting out as a first-time investment manager, be grateful for the leap of faith those early backers are making in entrusting you with their capital. They are effectively paying for some of your tuition. I'm especially grateful for the start I got.

Time dedicated to diligently practising the craft is the only way to bridge the *vicarious visceral gap,* though having access to one or more experienced mentors can help accelerate the process. Taking an

* Hermann Ebbinghaus pioneered research that supports the retention value of repetition and building on prior experiences.

† New managers do have the benefit of small size and some of the best track records have been in the first decade, so there are economic incentives to backing first-timers, it's just that the base rate is not as strong as it is for seasoned ones. And I should add in the spirit of full disclosure that when I've personally invested with other managers I've done so when they were starting out, as I enjoy being on the journey with them. Again, I'll choose good company all day long.

operating role in a business is also a way to bridge the gap. Any business will do. The real-world experience of what it takes to earn a dollar in a business environment massively enhances your ability to comprehend financial investments. The investment world and the business/operating world complement each other and spending time in the operating world before going into the investment world is time well spent.

While there is a wide difference between vicarious and visceral learning, the combination of the two is where practical wisdom is born. The vicarious knows 'what', the visceral knows 'how' and together they know 'why'.

Most competent investment practitioners are also prolific vicarious learners.* By constantly combining both direct visceral learning and indirect vicarious learning, thoughtful investors strive to be a little less ignorant every day and that is a far easier path than trying to be exceptional.

* There will be iconoclastic exceptions of course, especially in the world of trading.

To go even further add both reflection and writing to our vicarious and visceral learning. Wordsworth reminded us that habit rules the unreflecting mind. Simply taking time in silence, to sit, think and reflect seems more and more absent from our modern way of working, yet reflection is the bridge from knowledge to wisdom.

Using our own words when writing is powerful. When we translate what we've learned into our own language, it requires us to engage deeply with the material. This process forces us to interpret the information, reflect on its meaning, and then express it in a way that resonates with our own experiences and understanding. This active engagement helps to cement the information in our memory, making it easier to recall later. Furthermore, using our own words to document learning encourages us to make connections between new information and what we already know. Above all, personalising the learning process by using our own words can make the material more interesting and relevant to us. This increased interest naturally improves our motivation to learn and our likelihood to enjoy the journey as its own reward.

In an investment context, we don't really understand something unless we can write it down. You might think you do but trust me you don't.* It's no coincidence that many of the best long-term investors are also very good writers. They can translate their learning, experience, and reflections into clear language that demonstrates practical wisdom.

* There are life exceptions where our intuition knows more that we can ever articulate, but in investing, articulation and understanding are deeply intertwined.

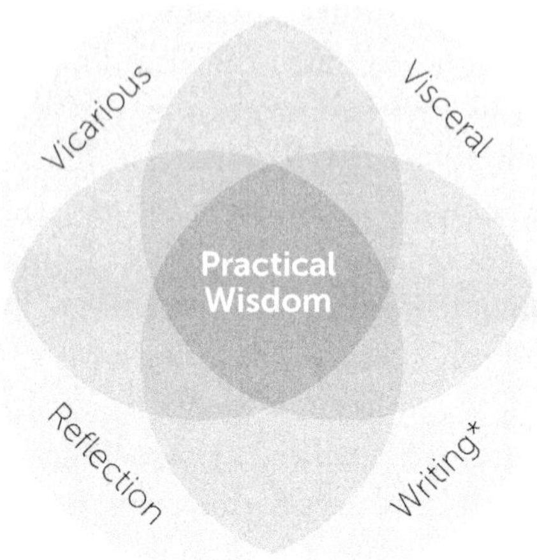

If we combine this multi-pronged approach to learning, then we will always be improving. If we are always improving, our best days are always ahead.

Conclusion

Deep learning takes patience and time. There are no shortcuts. Just because we have learned something at an intellectual level doesn't mean that we truly understand it. Understanding comes from direct exposure supported by reading, reflecting, personalised documenting, and contextual relating. The more we dig, the wider the circumference of our learning opportunity.

Exposure trumps knowledge. Facts can kill theories, but theories can't harm facts. Einstein said that "Any fool can know. The point is to understand." Don't bring knowledge to a wisdom fight.

* I learned a fifth step from Peter D. Kaufman which is to organise what you have documented. Put order on everything you document and look for the relatedness. Schopenhauer preferred a well organised small library to a large one in disorder.

21

Chapter Twenty-One: Designing an Asset Manager

If I had eight hours to chop down a tree, I'd spend six sharpening my axe.

– Abraham Lincoln

So, I'm guessing that after reading Chapter 7 you could be forgiven for thinking you wouldn't mind getting into the business of asset management? Well, so did I, and in this chapter, I share some reflections on the topic.

Let's assume you have done your investment management apprenticeship, have started to bridge the *vicarious visceral gap*, and are considering starting your own asset management firm. What things are worth thinking about at the outset, that if you got them right, would increase your chances of sustainable success? Expressed differently, how does one create structural competitive advantages in an asset management business? The cornerstone should align with client interests, primarily reflected through sustained investment performance. The revised question then becomes: Apart from the essential skill of rationally allocating capital, what structural elements can an investor implement to enhance long-term outcomes?

1. Permanent Capital. In the hands of a competent capital allocator, having permanent capital is a tremendous competitive advantage. The best opportunities frequently occur when the typical investor behavioural bias is to redeem and head for the safe refuge of holding cash. This is why average investor returns are significantly lower than the average mutual fund returns, i.e. investor level returns are worse than fund-level returns due to poor timing decisions. Fund redemptions are high when prices fall, and fund subscriptions are high when prices rise, which is precisely the opposite of what a value-oriented philosophy would suggest. In 2009, some of the world's best capital allocators missed the opportunity of a lifetime, and, by definition, so did their investors, as redemption notices turned up when the rational behaviour would have been to stay invested, or to increase allocations to risk assets. Having permanent capital allows capital allocators to:

a) At least maintain holdings/stay the course, or better, increase exposure, in times of market stress.
b) Focus on the long term when making investment decisions.
c) Concentrate their time on investing.

2. Flexible Investment Mandate. The expected returns from asset classes are continuously changing. Having the ability to go where the value is makes strong sense. In the hands of a rational investor (that knows their circle of competence), such flexibility is a clear structural advantage. To limit a mandate is analogous to boxing with one hand tied behind your back, or fishing in a puddle.

3. Tax Efficacy. We covered this topic in Chapter 3 so won't repeat it here other than to re-iterate two key points:

- Tax is a significant drag on long-term returns.
- We need to consider taxes at both the investment vehicle level and the investor level.

Tax is a specialist topic where professional advice should be taken, but generally, it is structurally advantageous to have investment funds/firms that:

i. Allow gross roll-up, or capital accumulation at low tax rates; and
ii. Deliver their returns to investors in the form of capital gains rather than as income.

4. Low Costs. An investment fund/firm that has low costs has a structural advantage. This is especially evident in low return environments. Fair asset management fees, low asset turnover and a simple fund/firm structure all help to keep costs in check.

5. Alignment of Interest. Given the critical importance of incentives, investment firms where the managers have most of their wealth invested alongside outside investors can be a competitive advantage in that it addresses the agency problem and results in a more focused investment effort.*

6. Communication. From my very first quarterly letter I decided that I would aspire to communicate in a way that was timely, transparent, and thoughtful.† The first of these two are entirely in our own control and the third is a continual work in progress.

7. Other Competitive Advantages. Some people argue that being away from the major financial centres is a competitive advantage. We don't have enough statistical evidence to tell. It at least seems clear that operating outside New York or London is not an impediment to investment performance.

* One may argue that this is more in the nature of good housekeeping than a structural/competitive advantage, and the research here is somewhat divided.

† Since inception I have always reported within a couple of days of each quarter end. This may not technically qualify as a competitive advantage, but it shows a healthy degree of earnestness. You may have also noticed that the better listed companies are more prompt in their reporting.

Companies like Berkshire Hathaway, Fairfax and Markel have most if not all the above structural advantages, though the tax drag is arguably higher than if those companies were domiciled elsewhere. Leucadia (before its combination with Jefferies) had all of them (securing its tax efficacy by starting out with a corporation that had substantial tax loss carry forwards).

Conclusion

If you want to become an asset manager, think beyond your capabilities as an investment manager. Consider the design and structures of the business itself and align everything in service of clients, resilience, efficiency, flexibility and longevity.

22

Chapter Twenty-Two: Hard to Beat

One of the symptoms of an approaching nervous breakdown is the belief that one's work is terribly important.

– Bertrand Russell

OK, so you like the economics of asset management, have decided to become an asset manager yourself, and have set yourself up in a structurally advantaged way. Wonderful. Just be aware that you have tough competition, not only from other managers, for here stands the rarely defeated beast that is the S&P 500 index.

Investment managers like to feel they are doing important work. Yet it is widely known that most investment managers fail to beat a passive investment in the S&P 500 (when measured over any reasonable investment time horizon). For professional capital allocators, this is both an irrefutable and inconvenient insight. It is an insight that is so inconvenient in fact, that most active investors, me included, swiftly proceed to ignore it. We battle the S&P 500, not for the glory of victory, but for the lessons in defeat.

Why is the S&P 500 so hard to beat?
I believe there are several reasons, some of which are well understood, and a few that have been given less attention but are no less important.

1. Low Cost. This is perhaps the clearest advantage accruing to a passive S&P 500 investor. Market-beating gross returns generated by good active investment managers are, in most cases, more than absorbed by the higher costs of active management.

2. US Capitalism is Effective. Capitalism and shareholder value have their opponents, but a better system (for investors) has yet to emerge. Respect for property rights, and in general, a clear focus on shareholder value are common characteristics of the companies that comprise the S&P 500. The disciplines of market transparency, potential takeovers, and shareholder activism all conspire to keep the focus on shareholder value.

3. Quality & Diverse Industry Capture. The S&P 500 captures a formidable combination of both quality companies and industry diversity. That said, there are times when the entire market is more concentrated than normal, and now could well be one such time, given the concentration of a handful of large technology companies.*

4. Tax Free & Low/No cost re-balancing. Constituents of the S&P 500 change. The stated gross return of the S&P 500 makes no allowance for the fact that in practice there are friction costs associated with portfolio churn. The 'friction-free' index return is theoretical only and doesn't exist in practice (though some of the largest index funds are getting close).

5. Limits Losses. Avoiding large losses is a prerequisite to wealth preservation. The typical S&P 500 company is diversified and lowly leveraged. Losing companies eventually fall out of the S&P 500 resulting in a soft form of automatic stop-loss protection.

6. Keeps Winners. How many ten-baggers have you enjoyed? We can be too eager to 'lock-in' gains, well before achieving a multi-bagger, relying perhaps too much on the idea that one never went broke taking a profit.† Peter Lynch managed this premature selling risk by constantly asking which inning a company was in. If it felt like early innings he held onto the stock (irrespective of how profitable it was as a holding up until that point).

* As of early 2024 it's 'The Magnificent Seven' driven by a supportive story around artificial intelligence. Choosing an equal-weighted version of the S&P 500, over the traditional market cap-weighted index, is one way to mitigate the tech concentration.

† Furthermore, the path to a ten-bagger is often punctuated with eye-watering valuations, that look crazy when viewed through a base-rate lens.

Over the longer term, of the total returns that accrue to the stock market, those returns are disproportionately earned by a small number of companies.* Winners contribute asymmetrically to total stock market returns. Owning *and keeping* winners is transformational. A holder of the S&P 500 *automatically keeps* their winners, and this is a big feature of why the S&P 500 is so hard to beat.

There is one further nuance that is worth highlighting. With all the accolades supporting index investing there is a key assumption that is fundamental to the index investment case, and it is this: Index investors buy and hold the index through thick and thin. This may be theoretically true, but it is frequently *not* behaviourally true. When it comes to investments in active funds, the average returns to investors are much lower than the average returns produced by those same active funds. The difference is down to poor market timing. Investors don't stick with fund managers. They sell after poor performance and buy after good performance which guarantees a result that is worse than what the funds produce.† If investors time active funds badly, why would they be any better at sticking to a passive S&P 500 investment? And if you don't stick with your S&P 500 investment then you are not keeping your winners.

* As mentioned in Chapter 4, this is a mathematical certainty in a world of high failure rates.

† The DALBAR studies are a good resource for anyone interested in exploring this further.

Conclusion

While active managers sweat trying to catch the waves, the passive take the tide's free ride.

If you decide to manage capital for others, through an active stock-picking strategy, know that you have a competitor that is cheaper and most likely better than you. That's somewhat sobering, to say the least. But don't be discouraged. There will always be demand for active managers as a large cohort of people don't want to follow a price-insensitive index. Furthermore, very few indices have come near the S&P 500, and it too will eventually have its time in the wilderness.

23

Chapter Twenty-Three: Investment Philosophy

> *The horseman knows the pleasure of working his horse at a slow pace. He leaves galloping to the frenzied knight.*
>
> – Philippe Petit

In acting as a fiduciary of capital, either for yourself or for others, it's worth considering *The Three Rs* by striving to be *Rational, Resilient & Resourceful.* If we can do a respectable job in each of these areas, then we will earn our keep.

First and foremost being rational is about avoiding costly mistakes. It is also about intellectual honesty, humility, seeking out disconfirming evidence, and a keen understanding of expected value. Rational investors ask themselves why they are seeing a particular opportunity and what the market knows that they don't. William Thorndike's book, *Outsiders,* gives an account of a small number of CEOs who built phenomenal value for long-term patient shareholders. The common thread amongst these extraordinary wealth builders was that they were all ultra-rational capital allocators. If there was nothing sensible to do, they did nothing. If there was something compelling to do, they did it in size.

Being resilient is about ensuring we can stay in the game or being *durable by design*. Having a shareholder base with a long-term time horizon, (or even better having access to permanent capital), is a fundamental tenet of being *durable by design*. Aligned institutional culture and reward systems are also critical elements of building a resilient investment approach.

Being resourceful is about working as intelligently as one can to uncover interesting investment opportunities. Great opportunities are rare. By definition, they are difficult to find. Improving one's resourcefulness is a permanent work in progress. It's a journey of continually experimenting with finding ways to improve how one allocates the greatest amount of time to the most promising opportunities.

In keeping with the alliterative theme of *The Three Rs* to aspire to, I also have *The Three Ss* to avoid:

1. Don't be Stupid.
2. Don't be Shy.
3. Don't be Stubborn.

Hopefully, these need no elaboration unless you are shy like me. I continually need to remind myself that exposure expedites expertise. This is Sam Altman on the topic of exposure: " 'Give yourself a lot of shots to get lucky' is even better advice than it appears on the surface. Luck isn't an independent variable but increases super-linearly with more surface area–you meet more people, make more connections between new ideas, learn patterns, etc."

Everyone has their personal investment philosophy which develops over time. As we age and mature as investors, I think that we increasingly substitute reflection for action. My current thoughts from everything I've learned, experienced, reflected upon, written about, and categorised are:*

1. Sensible investing is the long-term harnessing of the power of compounding. Solve for survival and the returns will look after themselves. Duration is more important than the rate of return.
2. Investing is a partnership with company management. Insist on competence and integrity.
3. Be honest in your ignorance.† Avoid straying into areas that you don't or can't know.
4. Do your own work and do it well.
5. Use an investment checklist and continue to develop that checklist over time.

* All from the perspective of an active stock picker with a focus on long-term survival. Other styles and approaches will have different lists.

† Do you have specific practices that routinely challenge your approach, like reading those you disagree with for example?

6. Assess new investments against the expected return from your existing portfolio which is your true opportunity cost of capital.
7. Focus your time on the areas that are most likely to offer dependable long-term post tax real returns. The opportunity cost of time spent elsewhere is high.
8. Be explicit in the few key assumptions that are the largest drivers of the investment outcome. Test those assumptions with rational sceptics.
9. Cultivate an options mind-set. Understand the options that you are explicitly or implicitly getting or giving. Treasure the value of liquidity and cheap call options.
10. Be leery of leverage, direct or hidden. Understand its power and its pitfalls. If leverage is a big factor, be conscious of the binary nature of potential outcomes and size positions accordingly.
11. Understand probability based expected value and the broad shape of the distribution of possible outcomes.
12. Aggressively monitor your existing portfolio.
13. Fight the psychological tendency to "lock in" gains by selling winners.
14. Continually ask where you might be wrong. Treat a non-negligible market loss as prima facie evidence that you are wrong and retest both your thesis and your process.

15. The market is there to serve you. Slow down and wait for compelling opportunities.
16. Strive to master the craft of rational capital allocation with a balanced blend of humility and ambition.

Conclusion

Design your own investment compass and let it be a mirror and a map.

24

Chapter Twenty-Four: Where's Dick Fosbury?

It's not that I found what I was looking for,
it's that the search just dissolved.

– Leonard Cohen

Richard Fosbury radically changed high jump when he introduced the world to the Fosbury Flop. His approach looked quite unnatural. But it *felt* natural to Fosbury, and it won him an Olympic gold medal in 1968.

This got me thinking about whether the investment management industry has had, or will have, any Fosbury-worthy innovators? To qualify I suggest that the innovation should meet four tests:

(i) The innovation has not been part of mainstream thinking.

(ii) It substantially improves upon existing results.

(iii) It becomes the default approach for most successful participants.

(iv) The effect is enduring.

Fosbury met all four of the above. His innovation was novel, better, widely imitated and has stood the test of time. If there was to be a *Fosbury Investment Memorial*, to whom might it be awarded? Who are the investment management contenders?

Two potential contenders spring to mind, Ben Graham, and Jack Bogle.

Fosbury Contender Number One – Ben Graham

Ben Graham is the father of value investing. Value investing was certainly new, it improved on existing results and the effect is enduring. But value investing has not become the default approach for aspiring investment managers. Why? One suggestion is that more professionals don't practice value investing because value investors can underperform for long periods and this tests both patience and career persistence.*

* There are definitional issues with the 'value' label. Growth is a component of value. But the wider point remains. Irrespective of investment style, everyone will suffer long periods where their style is not working well.

Fosbury Contender Number Two – Jack Bogle

Jack Bogle is the father of mainstream index investing. Passive index investing was certainly novel, and it substantially improved on the results of the active industry. It literally raised the bar. The jury is still out on whether it will become the default mode for most capital allocators and whether the results are enduring. Bogle's claim to the *Fosbury Investment Memorial* will ultimately be decided by the battle between the benefits and pitfalls of passive management.

Turning firstly to the benefits. On average, passive management beats active management consistently and comprehensively. As we discussed in Chapter 22, the reasons are two-fold. The costs of active management, by definition, make the average passive result superior to the average active result. This cost drag is exacerbated by excessive active fees and the immense difficulty in choosing active talent. The other advantage of passive is related to the distribution of returns. For some time now, the lion's share of positive performance is concentrated in a small number of stocks and the only way to assuredly own those stocks is to own the index.*

What about the pitfalls of passive? The main pitfall is that passive is parasitic. It only works if active is doing the job of price discovery. Ultimately if the weight of passive becomes too heavy it ceases to be effective.

Other Fosbury Contenders?

Not many come to mind, but I would love to hear

* Again, timeframes are important here and our Chapter 4 footnote to the Bessembinder study applies.

your suggestions. In a complex adaptive environment perhaps there can never be an investment innovation that passes the enduring test? Maybe such impossibility is germane to the nature of the industry itself? When something works in markets, it attracts the capital that eventually sows the seeds of its destruction.

Some industries have had innovative step changes that changed the core operating framework. Other changes have been cyclical. Take the bundling-unbundling trends for example.

Close contenders might include securitisation* (ratings accommodate different risk and time preferences), and the "two & twenty" private equity fee model most notably pioneered by KKR founders George Roberts and Henry Kravis.† Or Michael Milken's use of junk bonds and John Templeton's global investing lens?

One area that seems ripe for a Fosbury breakthrough is retirement financial products. It is a vast industry with limited innovation so far. We have seen monumental resources and attention directed at improving health span and lifespan, and ridiculously little on how individuals finance themselves during this newly found time. We have put money into longevity without putting longevity into money.‡

---

* It would not surprise me to see the emergence of a pure-play securitisation firm, i.e., one that can securitise any asset.

† Though there are references as early as 17th-century shipping deals that had 20% compensation for treacherous journeys. Those fees were fair considering the hazardous nature of the voyages.

‡ For example, target date funds ignore the term premium that can be harvested from intergenerational wealth.

Conclusion

Both the investment management and retirement savings industries are enormous markets with little ground-breaking innovation. For anyone that can offer a Fosbury-worthy step change, the prize is substantial.

25

Chapter Twenty-Five: The Compounder's Element

> *It is a bit embarrassing to have been concerned with the human problem all one's life and find at the end that one has no more to offer by way of advice than 'Try to be a little kinder'.*
>
> – Aldous Huxley on his deathbed

If you have made it this far and have enjoyed what you have read, then investing may be an area where you find yourself *in your element*. And, if that's the case, consider yourself one of the luckiest persons around. Investing is a craft that is as fascinating as it is rewarding. You will see the world with fresh eyes and meet amazing people along the way.

Returning to the origins of the four classical elements of earth, water, air, and fire, I wondered what might be the compounder's element? Of the above four elements none fully resonated.* Perhaps there is a better element? One that goes beyond the core four elements, an element that can illuminate the patient path. I duly scoured the periodic table and hereby christen neon as the compounder's element. Why neon? There are a few metaphorical character-

*Though my portfolio knows plenty about being under water.

istics that I think make neon an apt and memorable element to signal our patient path.

Firstly, neon carries the atomic number 10, which we can take as a reminder to lengthen our investment lens and to think in decades rather than in years or months. Thinking in decades allows us to benefit from the natural compounding value of people coming together to build and enhance productive capacity. Lengthening our investment lens leads to a clearer focus on business quality and durability.

Secondly, a 10 percent annual return is a pretty good number to work towards over the longer term. Sensible decisions are rooted in reasonable expectations. Reasonable expectations, grounded in long-term timeframes are the personification of the patient compounder.*

Then there is Neon's atomic symbol 'Ne'. Capital 'N' can be characterised as maximising duration (the N or the exponent in the compounding formula), lower case 'e' can be characterised as reducing errors.

* If you are excellent and/or lucky you can do better than 10%. But with sufficient duration 10% will deliver more than ample prosperity. Unreasonable expectations all too frequently beget unreasonable risk taking which ends in tears.

Ne = Max(N) duration, Min(e) errors: which gets to the core of long-term compounding that we discussed in Chapter 1. Maximise longevity (N) through error minimisation.*

There are other relevant characteristics. Neon is a colourless, odourless, and tasteless gas under standard conditions. Sounds like a boring value investor to me. More tortoise than shark.

Finally, and most reassuringly, neon is a "noble" gas, technically reflecting its exceptional stability and reluctance to participate in chemical reactions under standard conditions. Taking poetic licence, we can aspire to be noble compounders not swayed by the fast fashion of the day, and when the prosperity eventually arrives, we might consider how the proceeds are put to good and noble use. Investing can be financially rewarding beyond our dreams, and we would do well to heed Huxley's advice to be a little kinder.

Conclusion

Fellow, noble compounders, thank you for accompanying me along this patient path.

I sincerely hope that *The Compounder's Element* helps you on your investment quest, a prosperous one enjoyed in the warmth of good company. And, if the prosperity is elusive†, hopefully you'll find more than sufficient consolation in the joyful journey.

Before finishing this book, I was intermittently writing another one with the working title, *Pebbles of Reduction, Reflections on Misplaced Pursuits of More.* In the spirit of philosophical balance, and to book

* We also have the Compounder's "anti-element", Erbium, Er, Max(E), Min(r). All error, no return.

† Remember we can't control for bad luck.

end our journey, I've reproduced an extract from the introduction below.

"Here is a thought experiment. Imagine a line on a page like the one shown below:

This line represents 8 billion people in the world lined up alongside each other. On the far left is the most destitute, least fortunate person in the world. Perhaps someone living in abject poverty, or mental torment, or both. On the far right, stands the most enlightened, most accomplished, perhaps luckiest, person on earth. Now take a pen and put an 'X' on the line that represents where you might place yourself, all things considered. I'd wager that your 'X' is somewhere deep into the right-hand side of the line. For many readers it may even be indistinguishable from the outermost right-hand side. There we find ourselves on the lucky side of life's lottery, and yet, we often want to push a little more to the right. Many, if not most, of our problems come from people furiously pushing to the right when we should be looking left."

So, by all means let's take the path to prosperity. Take it with good company. And look left. Enough is a lot.

Postscript

As you reflect on *The Compounder's Element* it may at times seem like I've been vague or grey, but that's driven by an appreciation of context dependency (the nub is in the nuance). Investing is as much behavioural as it is mathematical. It's people all the way down. If you find yourself in violent disagreement with any of the book's principles that's quite useful too. You will have eliminated an approach that's not for you. Reduction is a valuable thing. If you are reading this after 2024, please be gentle! Specific company examples are likely to age poorly. That's the nature of capitalism. While the examples may have aged, the principles should stand the test of time. Readers may notice apparent contradictions. Kinder hands could see them as paradoxes or aphorisms. The path to clarity is paved with ambiguity.

Please forgive the seemingly abrupt philosophical turn at the conclusion. All economic crafts have a social context. As engaging and as profitable as investing can be, I've often harboured a residual feeling that there are more useful pursuits–thus the strong invitation to take the journey in good company, or moreover to *be* good company, and to be thoughtful with the fruits.

If you have read my previous two books you will have noticed a style that is succinct, at least that is my aim. In each case I went a step further and added what might be considered the epitome of brevity, the form we call poetry. And in keeping with tradition, I also do so here.

Elemental

At the birth of every great seed,
The indeterminable beats begin.

To name is not to know,
Anything you yearn to grow.

Gardens to be conquered,
Not tended, nor toiled.
Tightly gripped, loosely grasped,
Ever sought, never found.

Glory in the sunlight glimpse,
Perceptible pulses of possibility,
Eagerly sought by young minds,
Guided by grand thoughts.
It's only when the lone search fades,
That the communal shift begins.

Seeking not ends, nor means,
But the collective joy in a shared sense
Of everything life brings.

And the bittersweet taste of its inevitable end,
Nourishing the ground for a new seed to defend.

Appendix – Choosing an Investment Manager

If neither direct investing nor index investing is for you, you can alternatively invest with an investment manager. Even though I manage capital as a fiduciary I have also invested capital with other managers. In choosing an investment manager I would look for the following attributes:

- ✓ Complete integrity.
- ✓ A fair and transparent fee structure.
- ✓ Demonstrated passion for the craft.
- ✓ Proven ability over a sufficiently long period.
- ✓ An investment strategy in which they have deep competence, with a philosophy that can be explained clearly.
- ✓ An appreciation that part of their role is to help you manage volatility. Helping investors stay the course is a critical, and frequently underappreciated, source of value.

I would then spread my investment between at least three or four managers that meet the above criteria, ideally those with different investment styles, i.e. non-correlated. I've also observed that some of the most capable investors are not especially good at marketing and the converse is also often true, so don't be put off if a manager is operating a relatively small pool of capital – that can in fact be to your advantage.

If you do invest through other investment managers, it's also worth being mindful of how you can be a supportive investor. Outside not second guessing them, try not to panic, or show your panic, in bad markets, or in times of relative underperformance. Even better, increase your allocation. Support shown in tough times is truly treasured.

Printed in Great Britain
by Amazon

49459302R00136